Do-It-Yours UKULELE

MW00827697

e audio
al video

BY TERRY CARTER

PLAYBACK+
Speed • Pitch • Balance • Loop

To access audio and video visit:
www.halleonard.com/mylibrary

Enter Code
4293-9992-4437-1040

Front cover ukulele photo courtesy of Flight Instruments

ISBN 978-1-70512-217-4

Visit Hal Leonard Online at
www.halleonard.com

World headquarters, contact:
Hal Leonard
7777 West Bluemound Road
Milwaukee, WI 53213
Email: info@halleonard.com

In Europe, contact:
Hal Leonard Europe Limited
42 Wigmore Street
Marylebone, London, W1U 2RY
Email: info@halleonardeurope.com

In Australia, contact:
Hal Leonard Australia Pty. Ltd.
4 Lentara Court
Cheltenham, Victoria, 3192 Australia
Email: info@halleonard.com.au

Contents

Introduction

 To access the material indicated by the icon seen here, just head over to *www.halleonard.com/mylibrary* and input the code found on page 1 of this book!

Do-It-Yourself Ukulele is a comprehensive method and playbook to help you become a well-rounded and exceptional ukulele player. As the name implies, you will be able to learn ukulele at your own pace with the contents of this book combined with the included videos. This book starts from the very beginning—even if you just purchased your ukulele—then helps you to play your favorite songs, develop correct and solid technique, jam with the blues, learn how to read music notation and tablature, and have a great time. *Do-It-Yourself Ukulele* will be the most valuable ukulele resource you will ever own and one you can continue to refer to time and time again. So, if you're ready to become the ukulele player that you have dreamed of being, grab your ukulele and let's get started.

Pro Tips & Info
The ukulele is a Hawaiian instrument, but it has its roots in the Portuguese instrument the *braguinha*.

Getting Started
Parts of the Ukulele ▶

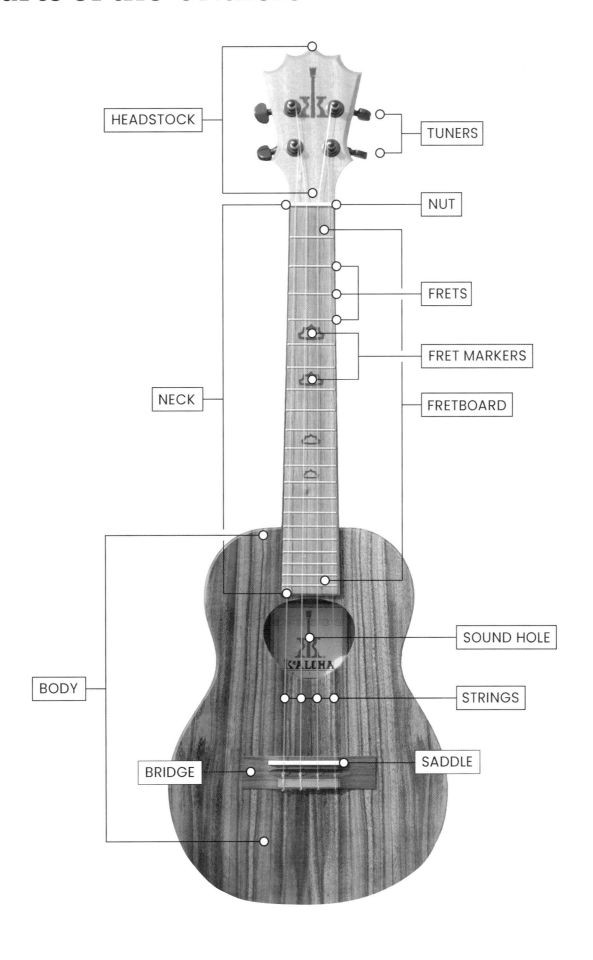

HEADSTOCK

TUNERS

NUT

FRETS

FRET MARKERS

FRETBOARD

NECK

BODY

SOUND HOLE

STRINGS

BRIDGE

SADDLE

Pro Tips & Info

- Ukuleles are made with many different woods including koa, mahogany, spruce, rosewood, acacia, and mango. Each wood has a different look and produces a different tone. Koa is a favorite used by most Hawaiian ukulele builders.

- Ukulele bodies are typically made with all solid wood, solid wood top with laminate sides and back, all laminate wood, and even plastic or carbon fiber.

- Most ukulele necks are made with mahogany for its strength and abundance.

- Ukulele strings are most commonly made of nylgut, fluorocarbon, and nylon.

Ukulele Sizes ▶️

Soprano   *Concert*   *Tenor*   *Baritone*

Pro Tips & Info

Baritone ukuleles are typically tuned D-G-B-E, which is different from the G-C-E-A of soprano, concert, and tenor ukes.

Open Strings on the Ukulele

These are the open string names for a soprano, concert, and tenor ukulele. The only difference between the high G and the low G is that ukuleles with a low G have a wider range of notes.

④ ③ ② ①

High G C E A
(or low G)

How to Tune the Ukulele

It's essential to know how to tune your ukulele, and it's not hard at all—especially with the aid of a tuning device or app. Watch the video for a full tutorial.

Pro Tips & Info

Reentrant tuning refers to a ukulele with a high G string; the strings are *not* ordered by pitch from highest to lowest.

Ukulele Hands

Numbers and letters are used to indicate which fingers to use for both your picking hand and fretting hand. These letters and numbers will show up in the music notation, tablature, and/or chord diagrams.

Fretting Hand

This is the left hand for right-handed players. The fingers are indicated in the music or chord diagrams with numbers:

1 = index finger
2 = middle finger
3 = ring finger
4 = pinky finger

Picking Hand

This is the right hand for right-handed players. It is indicated in the music with letters:

p = thumb
i = index
m = middle
a = ring

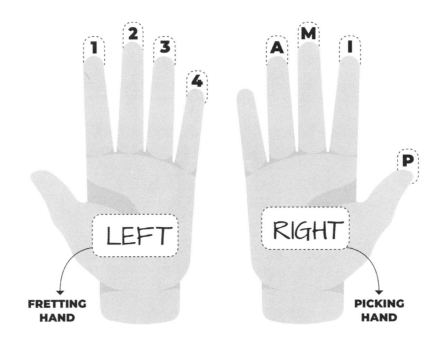

How to Hold a Ukulele

Holding a Ukulele Without a Strap

Holding a Ukulele with a Strap

Playing a Chord

Playing a Note

Strumming with the Thumb

Strumming with the Index Finger

Understanding Chord Diagrams

G C E A ← String names
4 3 2 1 ← String numbers
Nut →
Frets →
Strings

Name of chord
C
Do not play string → × ○ ○ ← Open string (no finger on string)
← Where to place fingers
3 ← Which fingers of the left hand to use

Pro Tips & Info
The ideal humidity for a ukulele is 40–50%.

Music Reading Basics

The Staff and Notes

It is important to learn and memorize these terms and symbols because they not only apply to the ukulele but to all music.

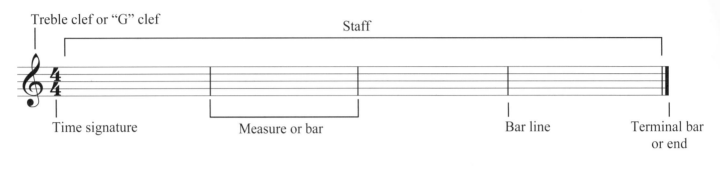

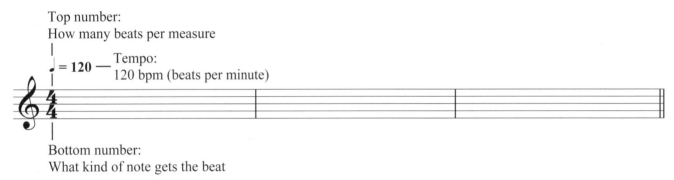

Notes on the Staff

There are seven note names in music (A, B, C, D, E, F, G), and they move up and down alphabetically on the staff. When notes are either above or below the five lines of the staff, *ledger lines* are used.

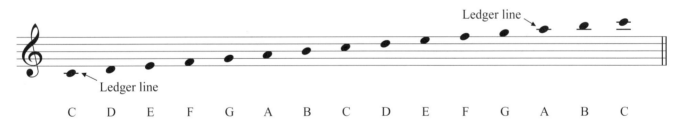

How to Remember the Notes

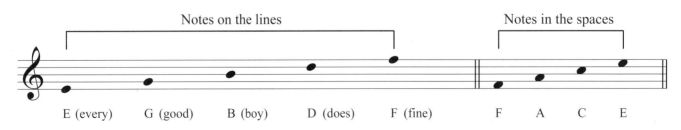

Essential Rhythms

The three main rhythms in this lesson are *whole notes*, *half notes*, and *quarter notes*. The way a note looks indicates its *time value*, or how long it rings out for.

| **Whole note** | **Half note** | **Quarter note** |
| rings out for 4 beats | rings out for 2 beats | rings out for 1 beat |

Rhythmic notation is used in these examples, indicated by the diamond-shaped noteheads for the whole and half notes and the diagonal slash for the quarter note. This type of notation does not indicate the *pitch* of a note (how high or low it is), just its duration (how long it lasts for). For these examples, you can play along with Track 1 again; pluck the open 3rd string (C) with your thumb.

A. This example uses all whole notes.

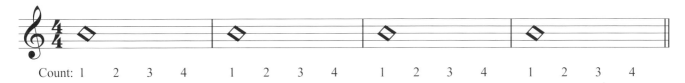

B. This example uses all half notes.

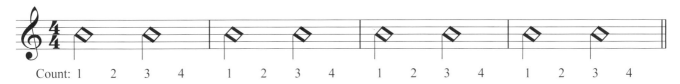

C. This example uses both whole notes and half notes.

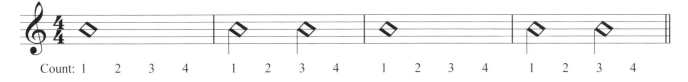

D. This example uses quarter notes.

Count: 1   2   3   4   1   2   3   4   1   2   3   4   1   2   3   4

E. This example uses whole notes, half notes, and quarter notes.

Count: 1   2   3   4   1   2   3   4   1   2   3   4   1   2   3   4

F. This example uses half notes, quarter notes, and a whole note at the end; you do not play on beat 2.

Count: 1   2   3   4   1   2   3   4   1   2   3   4   1   2   3   4

G. This example uses half notes, quarter notes, and a whole note at the end; you do not play on beat 4.

Count: 1   2   3   4   1   2   3   4   1   2   3   4   1   2   3   4

H. This example uses half notes, quarter notes, and a whole note at the end; you do not play on beat 3.

Count: 1   2   3   4   1   2   3   4   1   2   3   4   1   2   3   4

Pro Tips & Info: Accidentals

An *accidental* is a symbol that alters the note it precedes. There are three main accidentals:

   ♯ = *sharp* = raises the pitch by a *half step*, or one fret

   ♭ = *flat* = lowers the pitch by a half step, or one fret

   ♮ = *natural* = cancels the previous accidental

Chords: Let's Play Some Songs
C Chord (Whole Notes)

In this example, we'll play the C major chord using whole notes (four beats per measure) and downstrokes (⊓). (Note: When we refer to major chords, we just say the letter name—in this case, "C.") Use your thumb (*p*) to strum on beat 1 of each measure and let the chord ring out for four beats. Make sure to memorize the C chord and count out the beats.

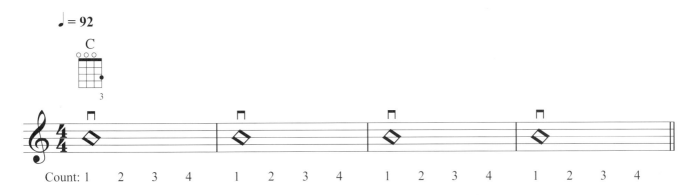

> **Pro Tips & Info**
> When strumming chords, play with a relaxed and loose wrist.

C and Am (Half Notes)

Now, we'll play C and A minor (Am) chords with half notes (two beats). Each chord is fretted with only one finger, and we'll strum on beats 1 and 3. Switching between the chords becomes easier with practice and memorization. Use your thumb to strum.

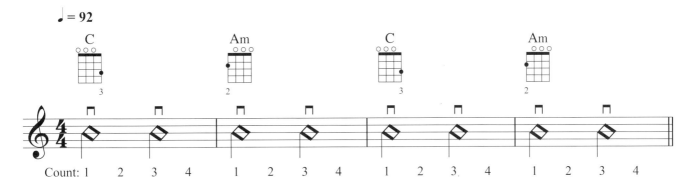

> **Pro Tips & Info**
> Major chords sound happy and bright, while minor chords sound dark and sad.

Am and F (Quarter–Quarter–Half)

This lesson adds the F chord to the Am chord. The rhythm is quarter note–quarter note–half note, which means you will strum on beats 1, 2, and 3, and then let the chord ring out over beat 4. A simple trick is to keep your 2nd finger down on the 4th string for both chords. Use your index finger to strum.

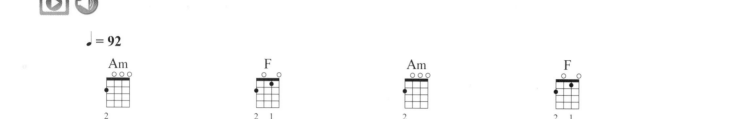

Count: 1 2 3 4   1 2 3 4   1 2 3 4   1 2 3 4

G7 Chord (C–G7 Progression)

Our next example on the following page uses repeat signs. You are supposed to repeat whatever music is between the beginning and end repeat signs. If there is no beginning repeat sign, go back to the beginning of the piece of music and repeat from there.

This is the chorus of the Beatles song "Yellow Submarine," which uses only the C and G7 chords. We'll use a simple quarter-note rhythm: four downstrokes each measure, played with our index finger. Get used to the G7 to C transition as it is one of the most common chord progressions in ukulele music. (Note: The lyrics are included if you want to try to sing along.)

YELLOW SUBMARINE
Words and Music by John Lennon and Paul McCartney

♩ = 102

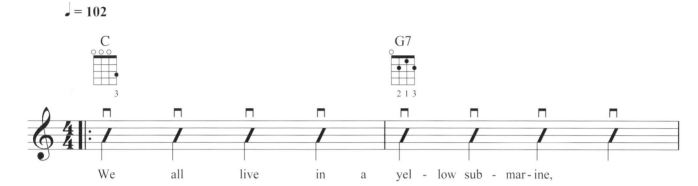

We all live in a yel - low sub - mar - ine,

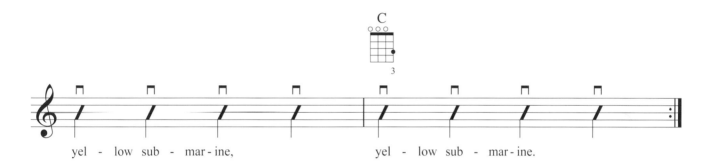

yel - low sub - mar - ine, yel - low sub - mar - ine.

Pro Tips & Info
For the best sound, strum the strings of your ukulele where the neck and body meet.

G Chord (Two Chords per Measure)

Let's stick with a winning formula and do another Beatles song. "Let It Be" includes the G chord and has two chords in each measure. The chords in this song are the most important chords for beginners to learn on the ukulele.

LET IT BE

Words and Music by John Lennon and Paul McCartney

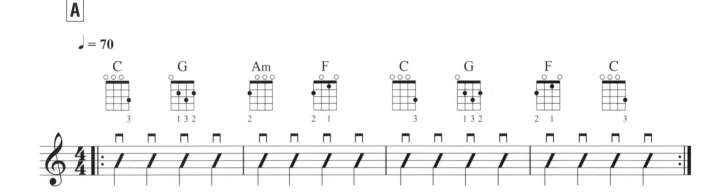

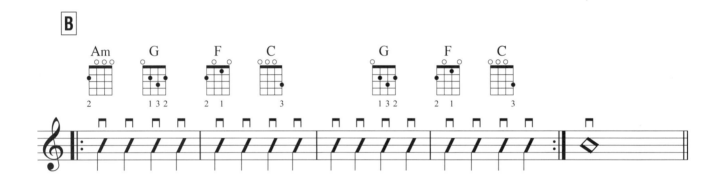

Pro Tips & Info

Switching chords is easier once you get the chords memorized.

Music Reading:
1st-String Notes (Open Position)

By *open position*, we mean the first three frets on the uke, including the open strings. Although we will learn to read some notes higher on the neck later, for now, we will focus on the notes in open position.

We'll start with the A, B, and C notes on the 1st string, or the A string. The A note is the 1st string played open (no fingers). The B note is on the 2nd fret and is played with the 2nd finger. The C note is on the 3rd fret and is played with the 3rd finger.

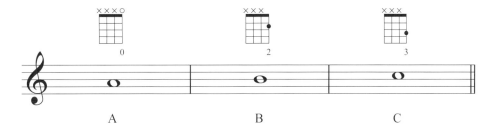

> **Pro Tips & Info**
> Reading standard music notation may seem hard at first, but the benefits of learning it will outweigh the struggles.

Example 1—Whole Notes

This exercise uses the A, B, and C notes, and they are all played as whole notes. The note names have been written under each note to help you get started.

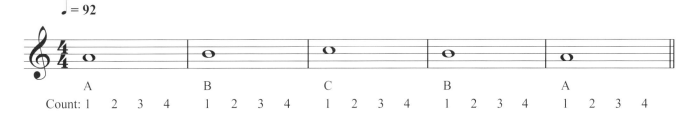

Example 2—Half Notes

This example uses mainly half notes. Notice the first note is C, and the repeat signs tell us to play the example twice.

Example 3—Quarter Notes

This example uses all quarter notes and has repeat signs.

> **Pro Tips & Info**
> When first learning to play the ukulele, your fingertips may hurt. This is normal, and once you form some calluses on your fingers, you will find it easier to fret notes.

This song uses all half notes.

SPACE CADET

This melody uses quarter notes and half notes and is played twice.

BEAN SPROUT

This song will help you master the difference between the quarter note and the eighth note.

SLINGSHOT

Need-to-Know Rhythms

The strum patterns you will learn in this lesson include whole notes, half notes, quarter notes, and eighth notes. In case you need a review, here they are shown with slashes:

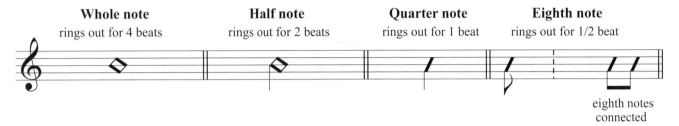

Whole note	Half note	Quarter note	Eighth note
rings out for 4 beats	rings out for 2 beats	rings out for 1 beat	rings out for 1/2 beat

eighth notes connected

The Five Mighty Strum Patterns

We will play these strum patterns using only a C chord, and we will play them at a tempo of 80 bpm. In addition, on the eighth notes, we'll use downstrokes on the *downbeats* (the numbers: 1, 2, 3, 4) and upstrokes on the *upbeats* between the numbers (the + or "ands").

> **Downstroke:** ⊓
> **Upstroke:** V

Strum Pattern 1

Use a down-up strum pattern for the eighth notes on beat 2.

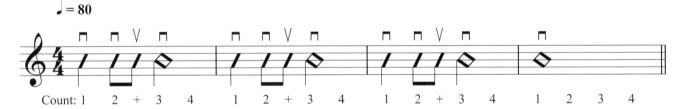

Strum Pattern 2

This pattern is the same as the previous one but adds a quarter-note strum on beat 4.

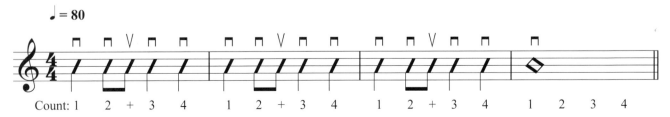

Strum Pattern 3

This one uses a down-up eighth-note strum on beats 2 and 4.

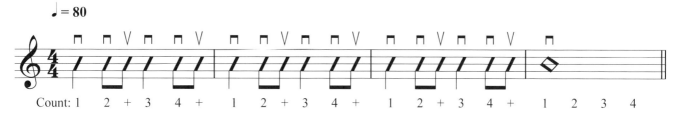

Strum Pattern 4

This pattern starts with a quarter note but continues with eighth notes on beats 2, 3, and 4.

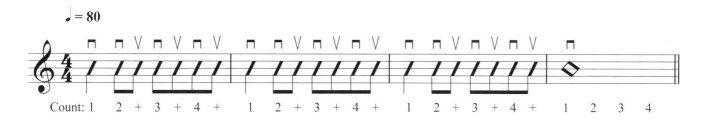

Pro Tips & Info: Ties

A *tie* is a curved line (⌒) that connects two notes of the same pitch.

- The value of the first note is extended by the value of the second note. In other words, you play the first note and let it ring out for the duration of both notes.

For instance...

- A quarter note tied to an eighth note lasts for one-and-a-half beats.
- An eighth note tied to another eighth note lasts for one beat.

Strum Pattern 5: The Island Strum

This important strum pattern is the same as the previous one, but the "and" of beat 2 is tied to the downbeat of beat 3. (In other words, don't strum on the downbeat of beat 3.) This pattern is known as the "Island Strum" or the "Granddaddy Strum."

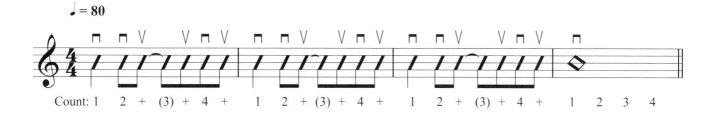

Pro Tips & Info

The Island Strum is one of the most versatile strum patterns you will need to master, as it works over almost any song.

How to Read Tablature

Now, we'll look at how to read *tablature*, or *tab*. For a full explanation, be sure to watch the video.

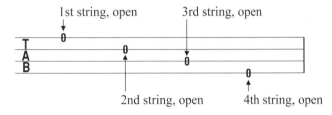

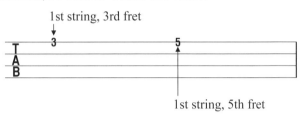

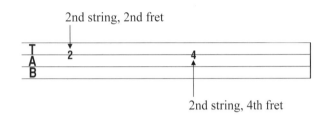

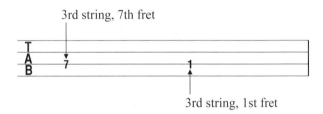

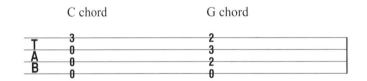

Pro Tips & Info: Dots

A *dot* adds half the value of the note it follows to that note.

- The *dotted quarter note* is a quarter note with a dot after it (♩.) and it receives one-and-a-half beats (1 + 1/2 = 1 1/2).
- The *dotted half note* is a half note with a dot after it (♩.) and it receives three beats (2 + 1 = 3).

This song will help you learn to read tab on the 1st string while playing a great melody. Normally, a standard notation staff would be shown above the tab staff, so you can see the rhythms and other important musical information. But since you're still learning how to read standard notation, for now we'll use a form of tablature called *rhythm tab*, which simply adds the rhythm stems to the tab numbers, as seen in the following songs. (Note: Ties are dashed in rhythm tab.)

LEAN ON ME
Words and Music by Bill Withers

♩ = 72

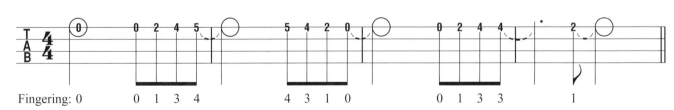

Fingering: 0   0 1 3 4   4 3 1 0   0 1 3 3   1

This song will give you practice reading tab on the 1st and 2nd strings. It is in 3/4 time, so it has three beats in each measure instead of four. Also, notice the *pickup measure* that appears before the first full measure of music. This is described in the video.

LULLABY
By Johannes Brahms

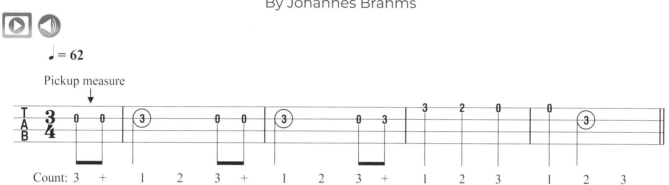

This fun riff by the Rolling Stones will help you read tab on the 3rd string.

(I CAN'T GET NO) SATISFACTION
Words and Music by Mick Jagger and Keith Richards

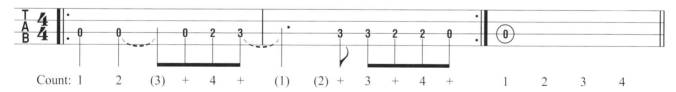

This essential song by Deep Purple can be played with either a high G string or low G string.

SMOKE ON THE WATER

Words and Music by Ritchie Blackmore, Ian Gillan, Roger Glover, Jon Lord and Ian Paice

 Low G Version

 High G Version

♩ = 110

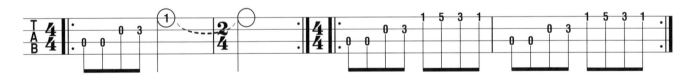

Pro Tips & Info

Owning a ukulele with a high G string and another with a low G string will allow you to play virtually any ukulele song.

This cool song by Roy Orbison uses strings 1–3. Notice the measure of 2/4, which means that one measure has only two beats; the rest are in 4/4.

OH, PRETTY WOMAN

Words and Music by Roy Orbison and Bill Dees

♩ = 106

Pro Tips & Info

Learning to understand and read tab will allow you to play more difficult music.

Strumming with the Upstroke

This "down, down-up," or "D D-U," strum pattern (D = down; U = up) is an absolute must for a ukulele player. It is Strum Pattern 3 from the Need-to-Know Rhythms section. Once mastered, it can be used in hundreds of different songs. This popular C–F–G7 chord progression is also a staple in many different musical styles. Use your index finger to strum.

TWIST AND SHOUT

Words and Music by Bert Russell and Phil Medley

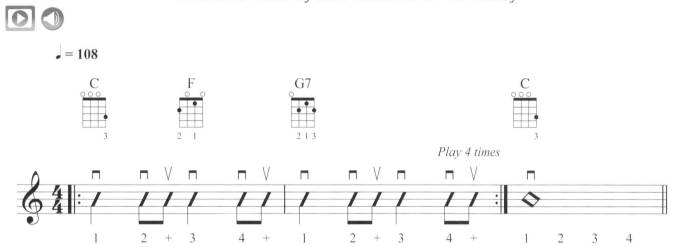

This song is a great example of how you can take the C, F, and G7 chords and make them into something different and interesting. The strum pattern used is Strum Pattern 4 from the Need-to-Know Rhythms section: D D-U D-U D-U.

LAVA
from LAVA
Music and Lyrics by James Ford Murphy

Verse ♩ = 116

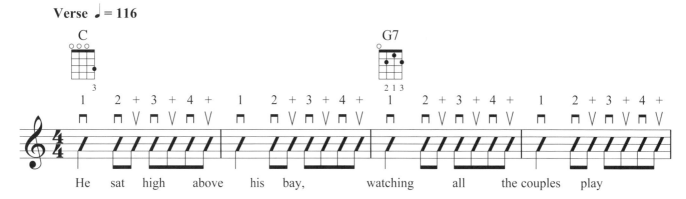

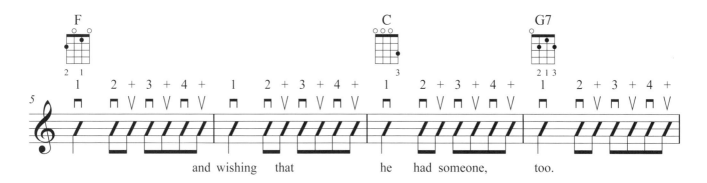

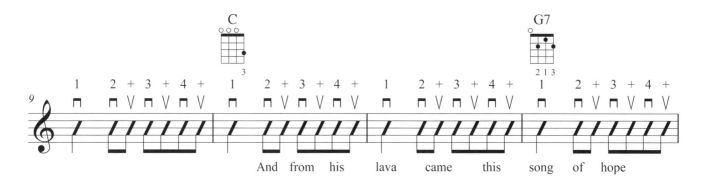

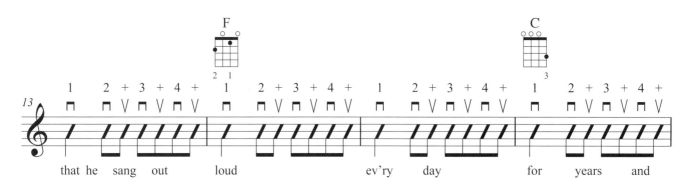

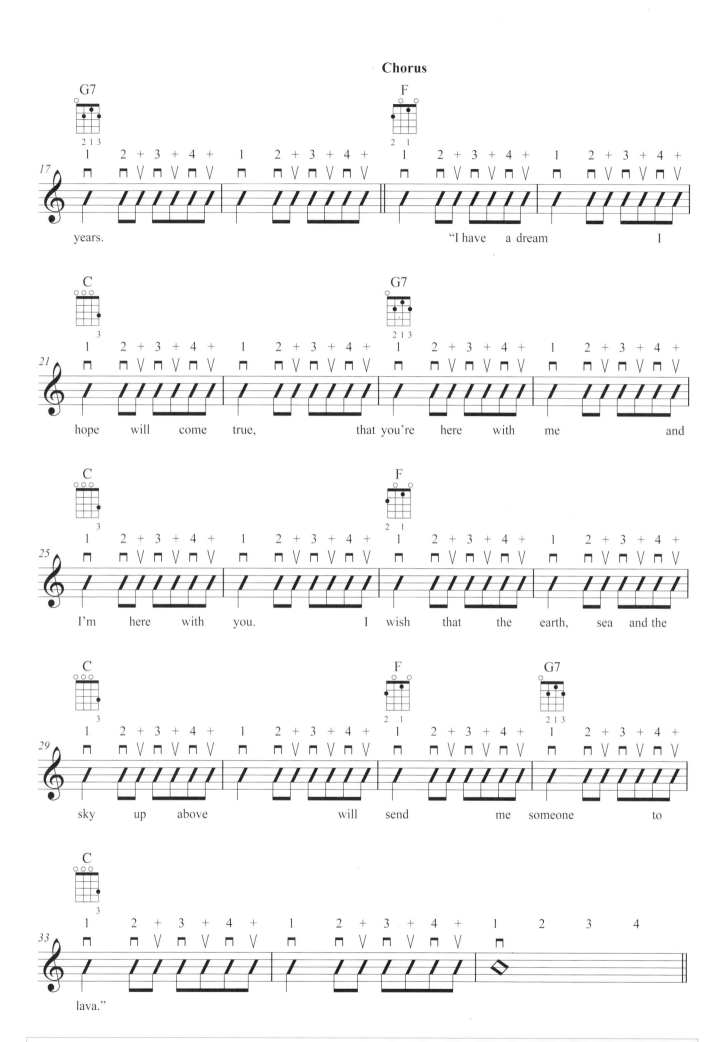

Technique Builder 1

This exercise is a great warm-up. It is also a great speed and technique builder for both the left and right hands. To play it, you will use fingers 1, 2, 3, and 4 and change to different strings as you move up the fretboard.

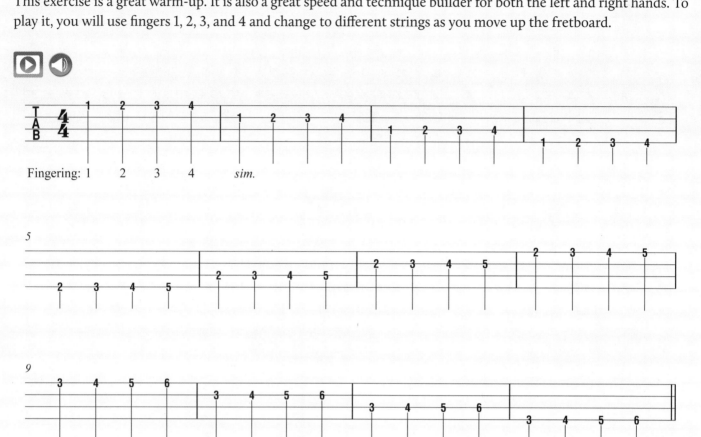

Pro Tips & Info

Don't overlook the simple things. They may seem basic, but greatness happens when you master the fundamentals.

Fingerpicking: *p–i*

This entire song uses an alternating *p–i* fingerpicking pattern (*p* = thumb; *i* = index). In the last measure, you will use a *pinch* to play the 1st and 3rd strings together. (We'll talk more about the pinch later.)

SUMMER SOLSTICE

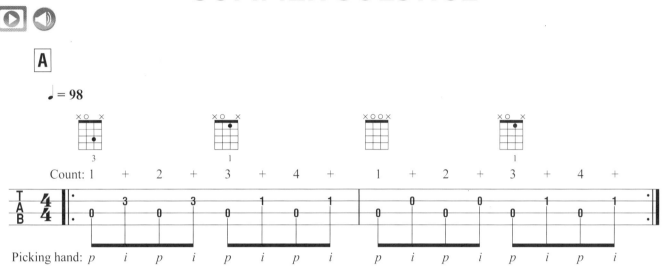

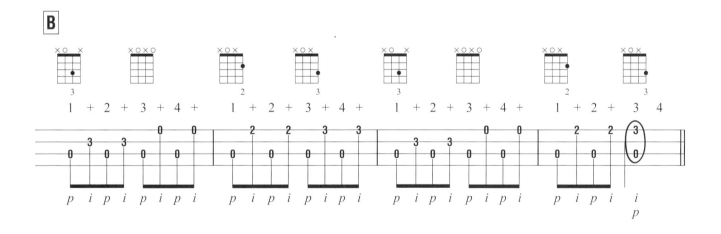

Pro Tips & Info

Playing accurately is more important than playing fast.

Music Reading:
2nd-String Notes

It's time to learn the notes E, F, and G on the 2nd string, or E string. The E note is the open 2nd string. The F note is played on the 1st fret with the 1st finger. The G note is played on the 3rd fret with the 3rd finger.

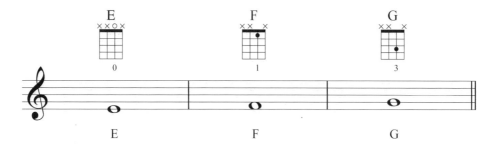

Example 1—Whole Notes

This exercise uses the E, F, and G notes and is played using whole notes. The note names have been written under each note to help you get started.

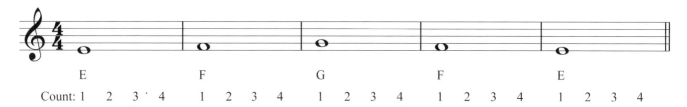

> **Pro Tips & Info**
> • Fret notes and chords with your fingertips so that each string rings out clearly.
> • Press your fingertips as close to the metal fret "wire" as you can (just to the left) without being on top of it. This will make it easier to press down the strings and will give you a better tone.

Example 2—Half Notes

This exercise uses half notes and has repeat signs.

Example 3—Quarter Notes

This exercise starts on the G note and includes only quarter notes.

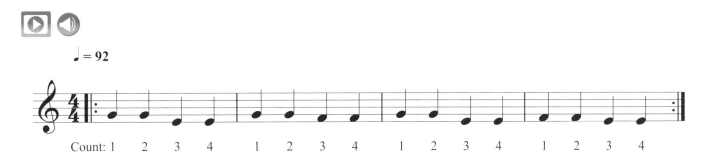

Example 4—1st- and 2nd-String Review

Here's a review of the notes on the 1st and 2nd strings using whole notes.

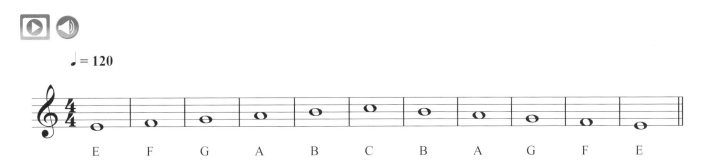

This blues song consists of notes on the 1st and 2nd strings. The chords are just included here for reference, or if you'd like to try this with another instrument playing the accompaniment.

LP BLUES

Here's another fun song featuring notes on the 1st and 2nd strings.

PIRATE'S COVE

C Major Scale

The *major scale* is an extremely important scale that many melodies are based on. It is also great to use for technique building and soloing. You can play the following C major scale on any ukulele tuned G-C-E-A, with a high *or* low G. (Note: Scale diagrams look like chord diagrams, but the notes are played individually instead of at the same time.)

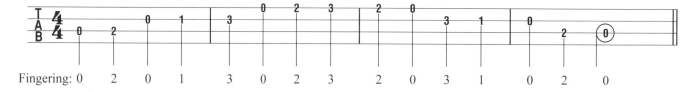

"Twinkle, Twinkle Little Star" is a great melody in which all the notes come from the C major scale. Aside from the melody, this piece is also great for practicing your chord strumming.

TWINKLE, TWINKLE LITTLE STAR
Traditional

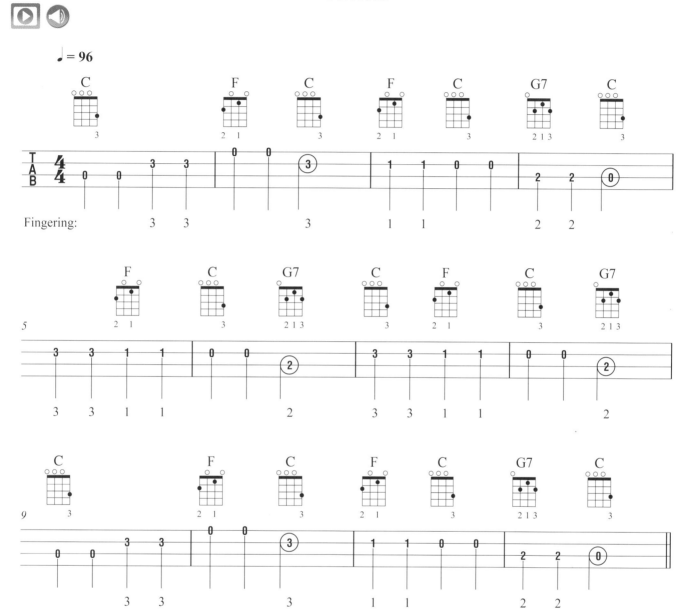

Chords:
The Island Strum

Let's use the chords from the song "The Wheels on the Bus" to practice the Island Strum (a.k.a., the Granddaddy Strum). This song uses only two chords, F and C7. The Island Strum has a tie on the "and" of beat 2, which means you do not strum on the downbeat of beat 3, but you do allow the chord to keep ringing out.

Notice this song also has repeat signs that include 1st and 2nd endings. The first time through, you play the 1st ending. Then, repeat from the beginning, skip over the 1st ending, and play the 2nd ending.

THE WHEELS ON THE BUS
Traditional

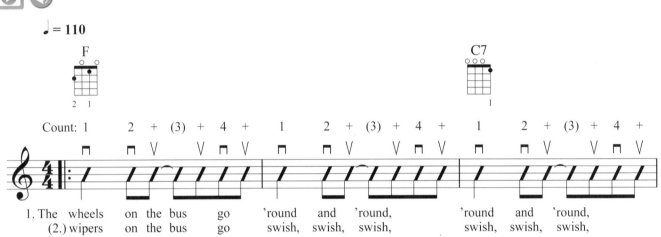

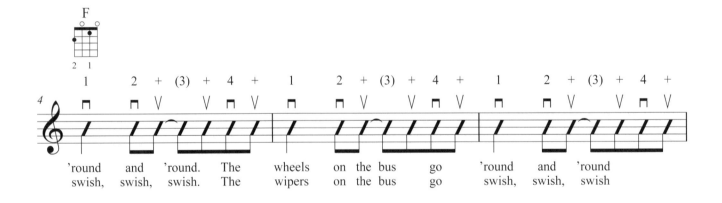

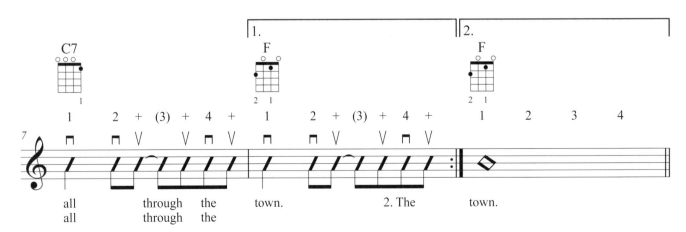

The middle section of Israel Kamakawiwoʻole's classic ukulele cover will help you master the Island Strum while working on the C, G, Am, and F chords.

OVER THE RAINBOW
from THE WIZARD OF OZ
Music by Harold Arlen
Lyric by E.Y. "Yip" Harburg

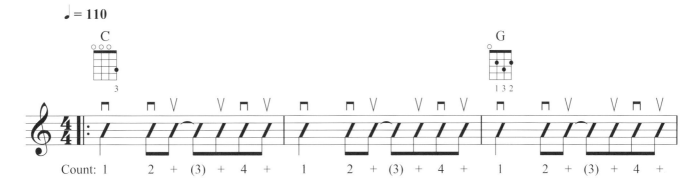

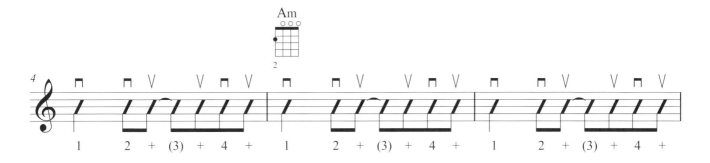

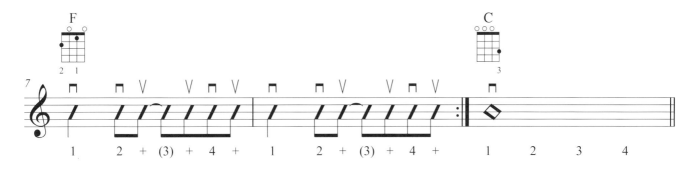

Now, we'll use the Island Strum on the common I–IV–I–V chord progression. For this song, the chords are G–C–G–D. The D chord is new, and there are several fingerings you can use, depending on what's comfortable for you. The fingering in the first D chord diagram includes a partial *barre*, indicated by the curved line, which tells you to press one finger (in this case, your index) down across the two strings under the barre symbol. Watch the video for an introduction to the barre technique.

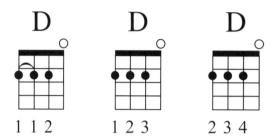

BROWN EYED GIRL
Words and Music by Van Morrison

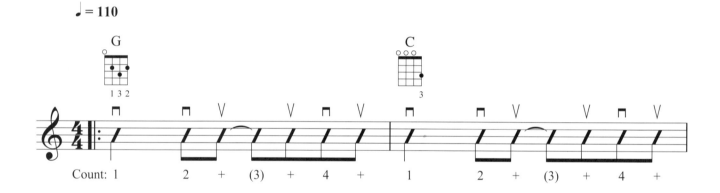

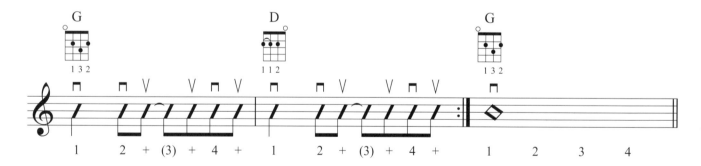

The Blues:
Part 1

In this lesson, we are using the Island Strum on a 12-bar blues in A. You will need the A7, D7, and E7 chords—three new chords!

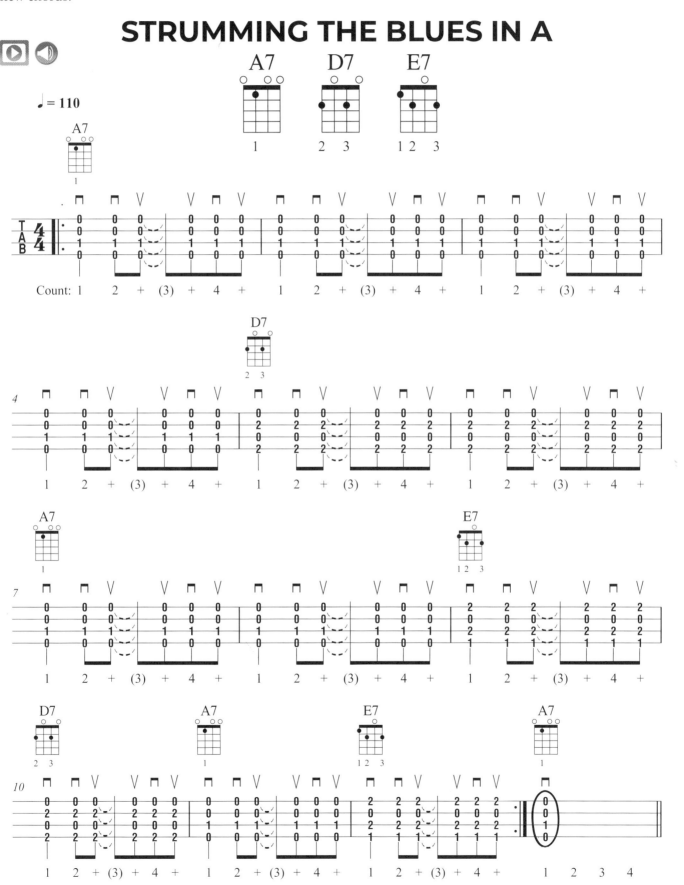

STRUMMING THE BLUES IN A

This next lesson is like the blues we just did, but we are going to add a *muted* strum (indicated with an "x" note-head) on beat 2, and a *quick change* to the IV chord in measure 2. Watch the video for a detailed explanation of both concepts.

STRUMMING THE BLUES IN A
(Mutes and Quick Change)

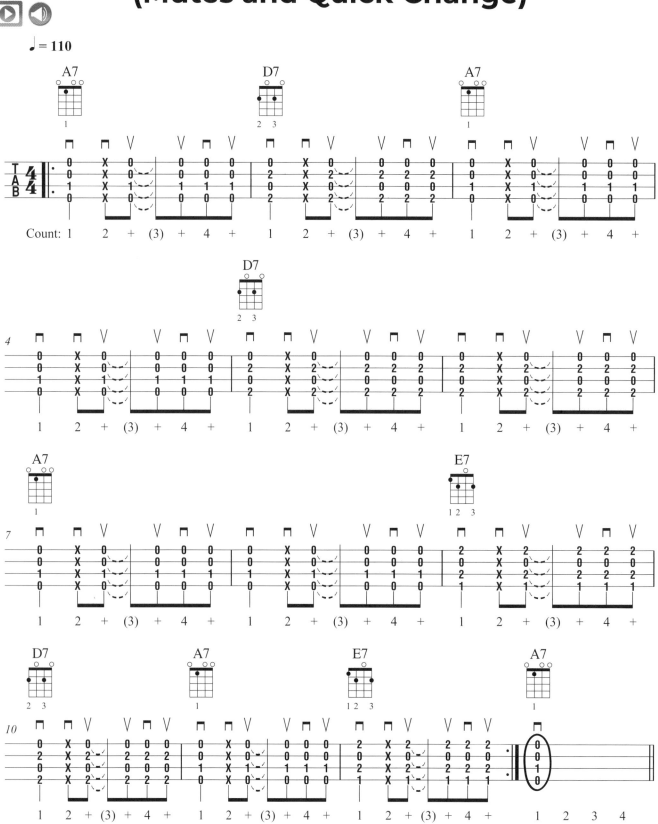

Technique Builder 2

This exercise will test your coordination and dexterity going from fingers 1 to 3 and 2 to 4.

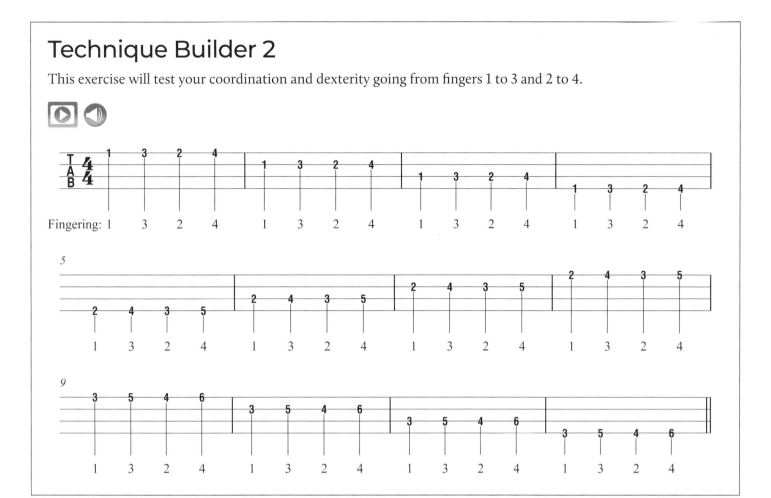

Pro Tips & Info

Daily practice of 15 to 30 minutes a day will increase your skills faster than longer but less frequent practice sessions.

Music Reading:
Strings 1 and 2 Review

Example 1

This is a review of the notes A, B, and C on the 1st string. It features a mix of quarter notes and eighth notes.

Example 2

Here's a review of the notes E, F, and G on the 2nd string. It includes eighth notes, quarter notes, and a half note.

This song is played on strings 1 and 2, and it has eighth notes on beat 2 of every measure. The chord symbols above the notes are the accompaniment and are just for reference. We are focusing here on your note reading.

KING'S COURT

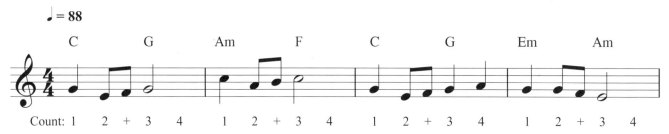

Fingerpicking Blues:
p–i–m–i

This blues fingerstyle song uses the *p–i–m–i* pattern (*p* = thumb; *i* = index; *m* = middle). It's a traditional 12-bar blues, but it has a cool ending and adds one more measure for a final whole-note chord. On the final chord, roll the fingers of your picking hand (indicated by the symbol 𝄉). To do this, start from the bottom of the chord with your thumb (*p*) and pluck the strings quickly one after the other (*p–i–m*).

LAZY DOG BLUES

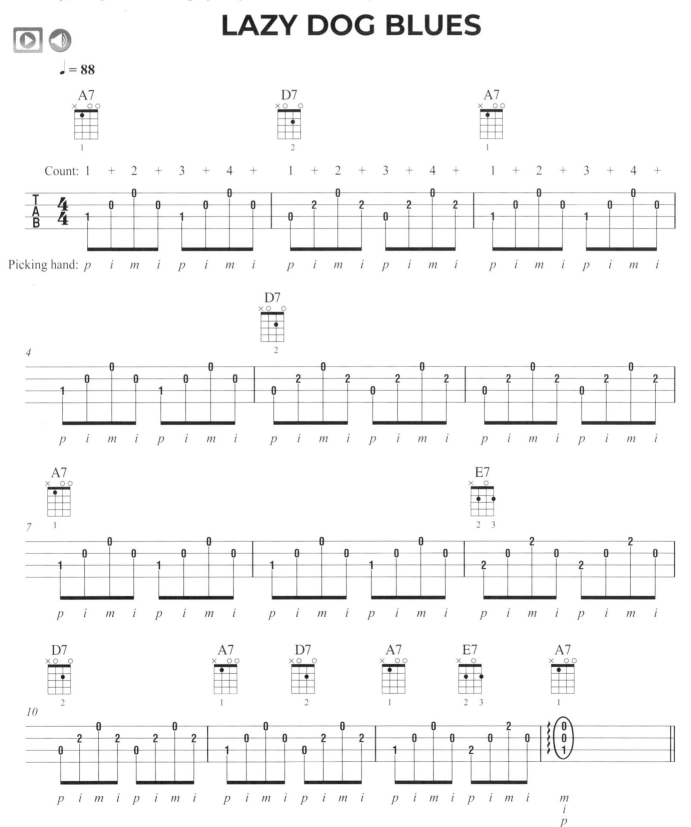

Chords:
More Strumming

"Aloha 'Oe" has a simple chord progression, and it is an absolute classic Hawaiian ukulele song. We are using Strum Pattern 4 from our Five Mighty Strums, but we will *accent* (＞) beats 2 and 4.

ALOHA 'OE (Key of G)
Words and Music by Queen Liliuokalani

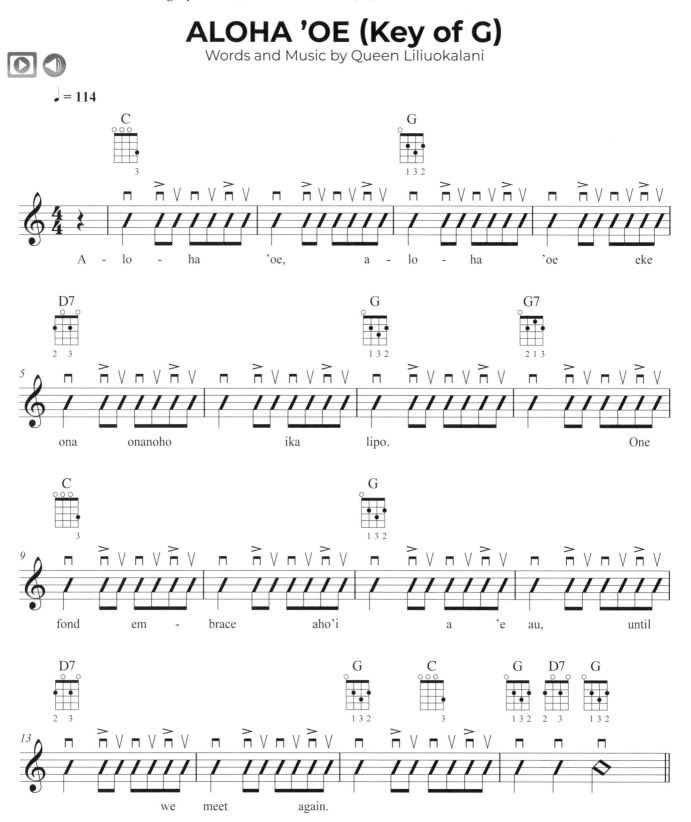

The Blues:
Part 2

Swing vs. Straight Eighth Notes

In this lesson, you'll learn how to count and play *straight eighth* notes and *swing eighth* notes.

You have been playing straight eighth notes up until this point. They divide the beat equally in half, so one note is on the downbeat (the number) and the other is on the upbeat (the "+").

To play swing eighth notes, you first have to understand *triplets*. A triplet is three eighth notes played in the time of two eighth notes, or one beat. A triplet has a "3" above or below it and is counted: 1-trip-let, 2-trip-let, etc.

Swing eighth notes are written like straight eighth notes, but they are treated like a triplet with the first two notes tied. In other words, you play the first note on the downbeat (1, 2, 3, or 4), hold it for the "trip," and then play again on the "let" of the triplet. In this book, the swing rhythm is indicated with the symbol (♫ = ♪♪) at the beginning of the music.

For the first example, we will compare the straight rhythm (written as regular eighth notes) to the swing rhythm (written as triplets with the first two notes tied).

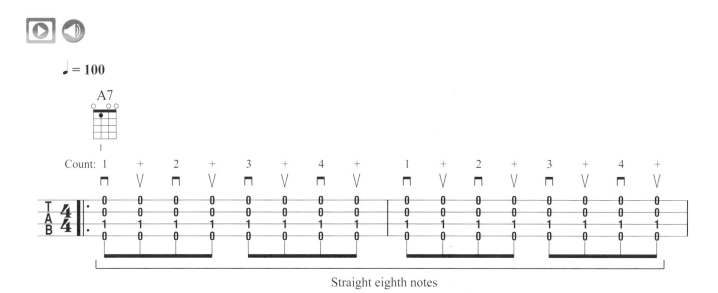

Straight eighth notes

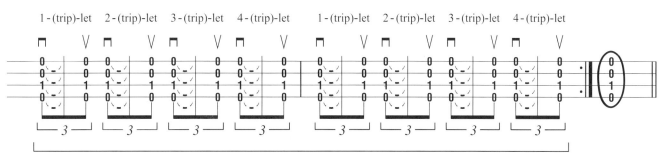

Swing eighth notes

Pro Tips & Info
Ukulele cases—both gig bags and hardshell cases—can protect your ukulele from damage.

Let's play a standard 12-bar blues with straight eighth notes. Remember, straight eighth notes divide the beat into two equal parts, creating more of a rock-driven feel.

STRAIGHT BLUES IN A

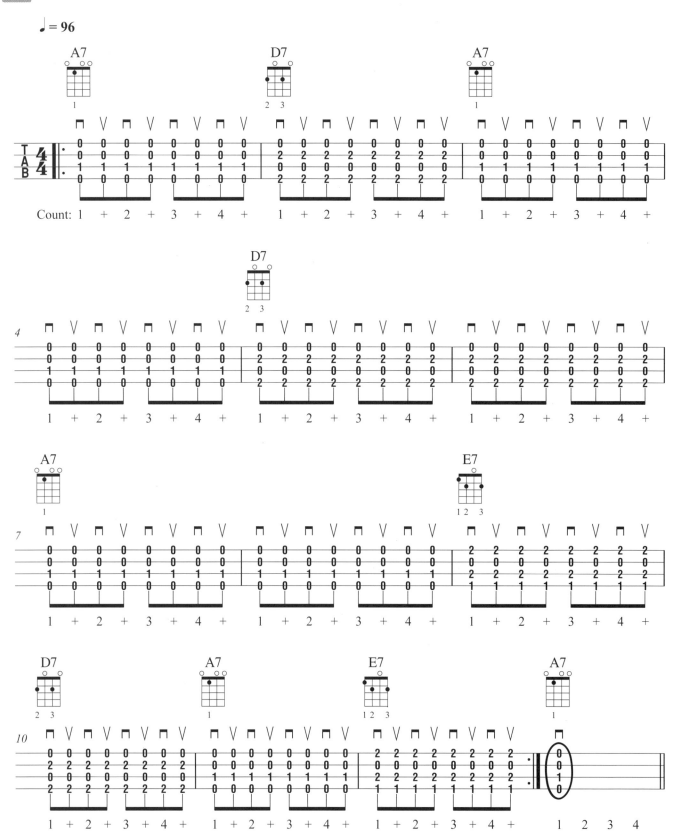

Although this shuffle blues is written like straight eighth notes, you will play it with a swing feel, as indicated by the swing symbol at the top of the music. Remember, to play in the swing or shuffle style, the first eighth note of each beat is held longer than the second eighth note. It's written like this because it's easier to read.

SHUFFLE BLUES IN A

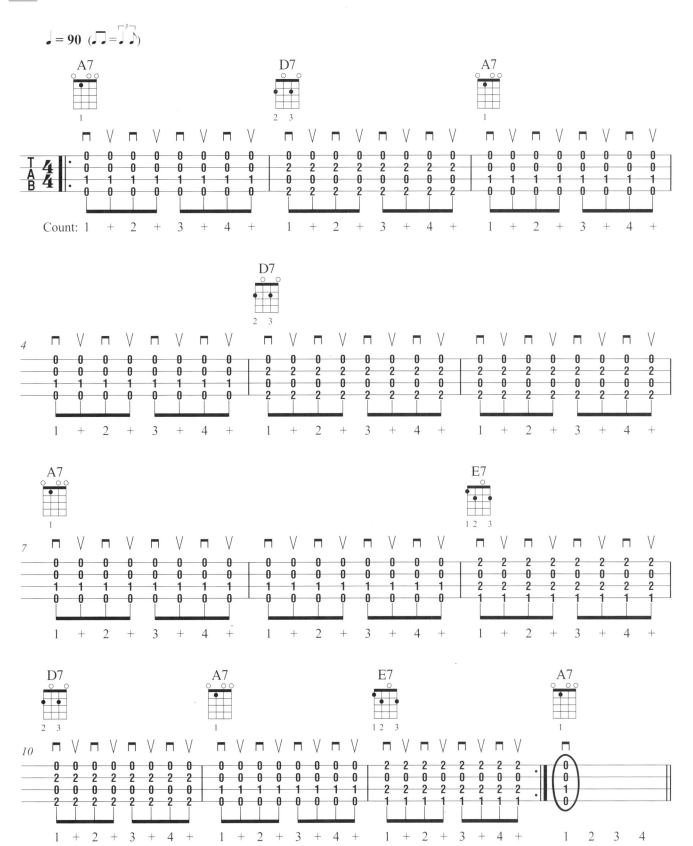

A Minor Pentatonic Scale (Open)

The *minor pentatonic* is a five-note scale, and it is one of most versatile scales you will learn. Besides sounding great over the blues, it works over many different styles of music such as rock, pop, jazz, and Christian. This example is meant to be played on a uke with a high G string, and the starting note will be the open 1st string. We call this an *open* scale form because it uses open strings.

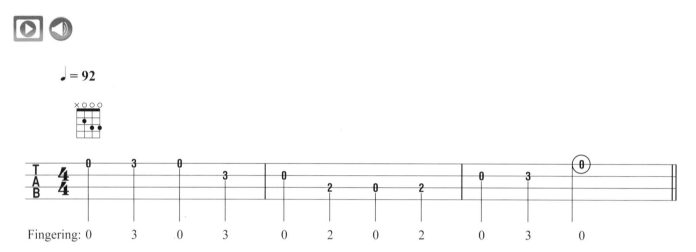

A Minor Pentatonic Scale (Closed)

Playing a scale in a *closed* position means there are no open strings. Even though this version of the A minor pentatonic scale uses the open 3rd string for the C note, we'll consider it closed because it avoids the open 1st and 2nd strings.

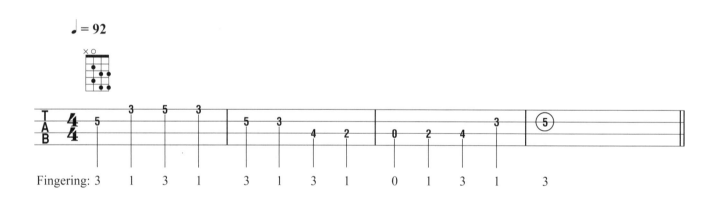

In this lesson, you will learn a cool blues solo based on the A minor pentatonic scale, but there's a twist. The twist is that there are a couple of bonus notes included: the E on the 7th fret of the 1st string and the D♯ on the 6th fret. The E note is part of the A minor pentatonic scale when you extend it up the neck, but the D♯ is a *blue note* and is part of the A *blues scale*. In fact, the A blues scale is the same as A minor pentatonic with the addition of that one note. Play this using swing eighth notes.

SHARK BITE BLUES (Solo in A)

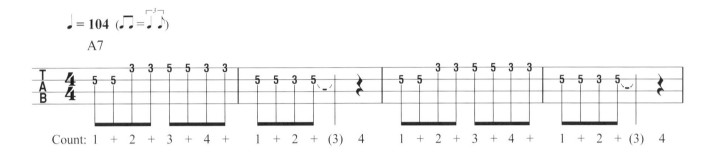

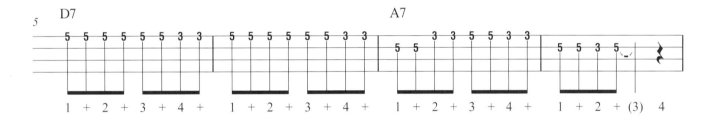

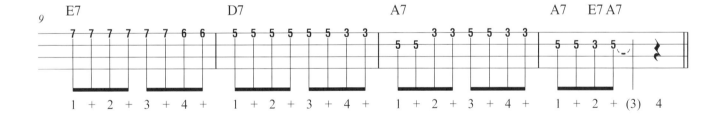

Fingerpicking:
p–i–m–a

This song uses the *p-i-m-a* (thumb–index–middle–ring) fingerstyle pattern. This is one of the most widely used fingerpicking patterns for both ukulele and guitar.

THE SHAKE OUT

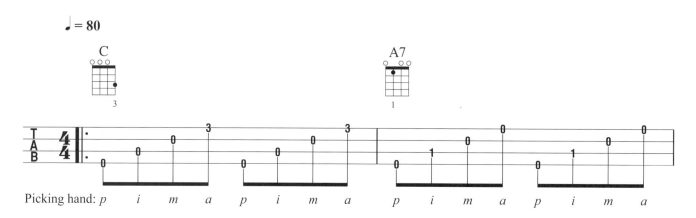

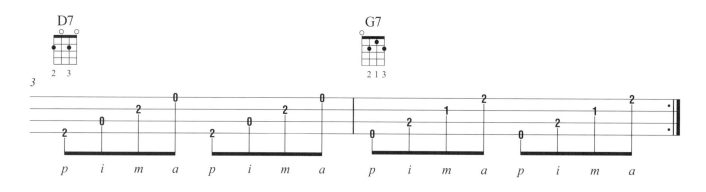

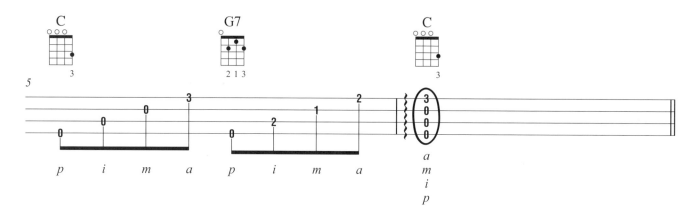

Let's use the *p–i–m–a* pattern over this classic chord progression. Although the C chord is written as a partial barre chord, you could play the easier open-position C chord if needed. In addition, there is a new B7 chord for you to work on. Note: There is a *ritardando* (indicated with "*rit.*") toward the end of the song. This tells you to gradually slow down the tempo.

(SITTIN' ON) THE DOCK OF THE BAY

Words and Music by Steve Cropper and Otis Redding

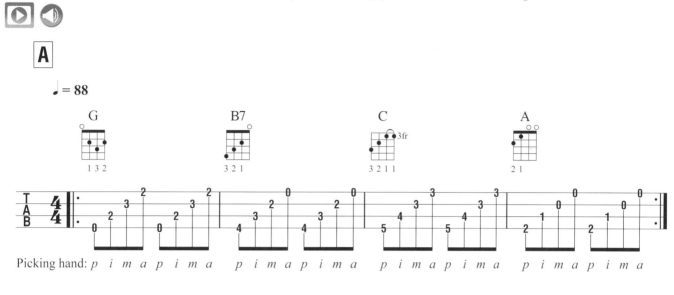

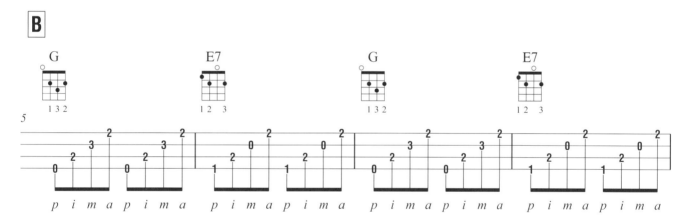

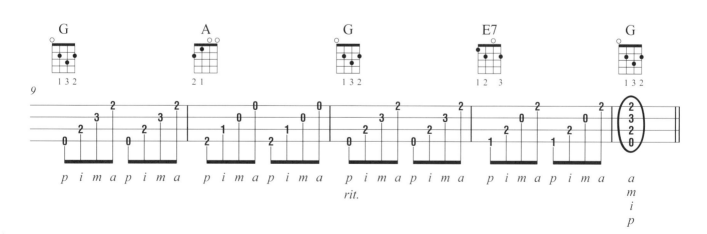

Music Reading:
Two-String Etude

This song will give you practice reading standard music notation on strings 1 and 2. Although it looks long, the 1st, 2nd, and 4th lines are almost identical.

BATTLE ROYALE

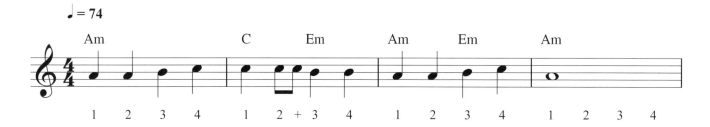

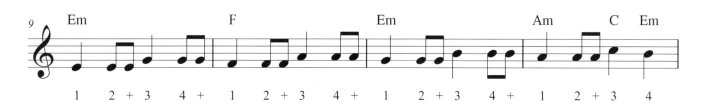

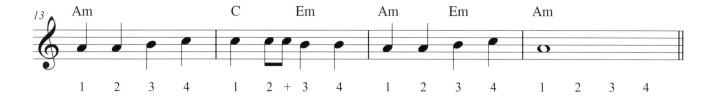

Using a Capo

We are going to look at how to quickly and easily change the key of a song, but first, we need to check out this great tune.

Here is the chord progression for the classic song "Stand by Me." This version is in the key of G major. It uses the Island Strum with a mute on beat 2. Remember, you create the mute on the "x" noteheads by hitting and resting the palm of your strumming hand on all four strings right before you strum the chord.

STAND BY ME (Key of G)
Words and Music by Jerry Leiber, Mike Stoller and Ben E. King

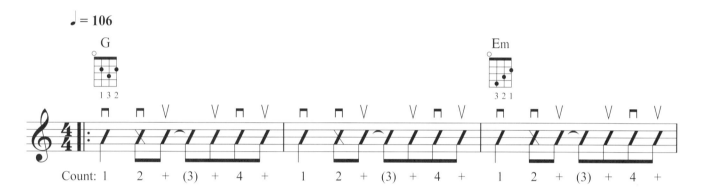

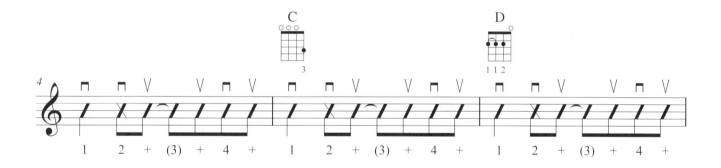

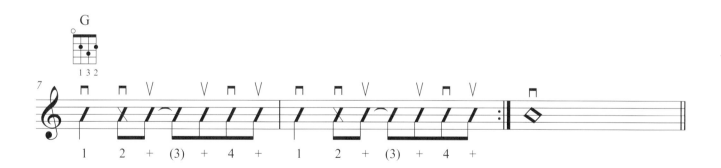

I'm going to show you a cool trick—how to use a *capo*. A capo clamps onto the fretboard and raises the pitch of the open strings, allowing you to play a song in a higher key without changing the chord shapes. We will use the same chord shapes as the previous version of "Stand by Me" in the key of G. However, when we place the capo on the 2nd fret and play the exact same chord shapes, every chord name moves up a *whole step* (the distance of two frets). The G chord becomes A, E minor becomes F# minor, C becomes D, and D becomes E. Cool trick, right? (Note: For the purposes of this lesson, we changed the chord names to the new key; but often, when a piece calls for a capo, the original key is notated and there is just an indication of where to place the capo.)

STAND BY ME (Key of A)

Words and Music by Jerry Leiber, Mike Stoller and Ben E. King

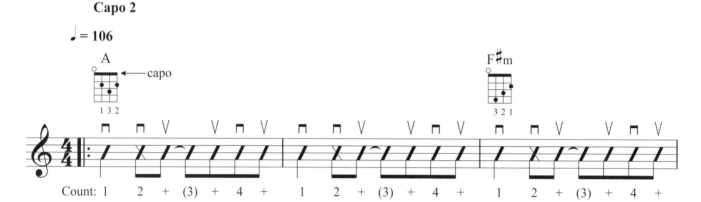

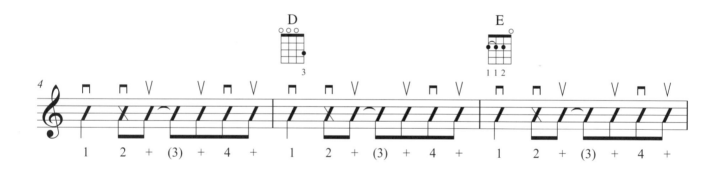

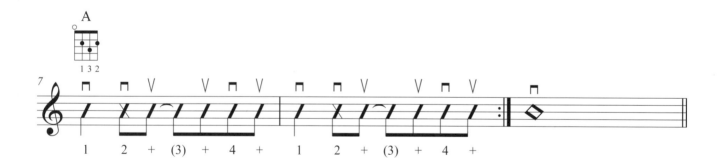

Pro Tips & Info

A capo is an absolute must for any ukulele player, especially if you are a singer or are playing with a singer. The capo allows you to easily change the key of any song and adapt to a singer's range.

Open Blues Shuffle

In this lesson, we will learn how to play a boogie woogie blues in the key of G. This is one of the most important blues patterns to learn, as many variations can later be applied to this. This uses a shuffle rhythm and open strings.

BOOGIE WOOGIE BLUES IN G

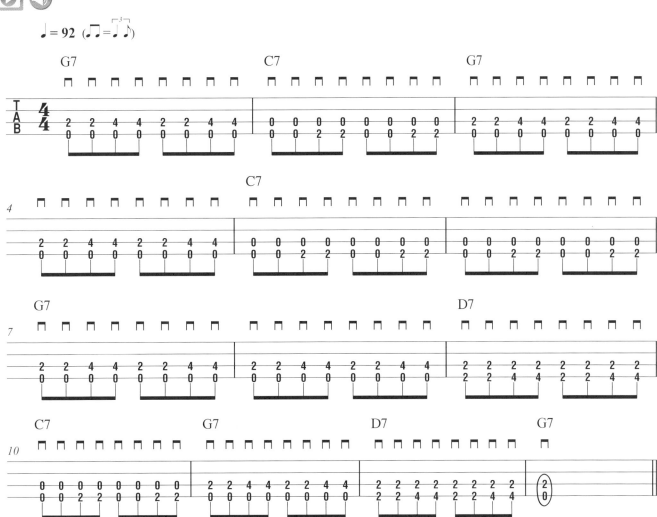

G Minor Pentatonic Scale (Open)

The G minor pentatonic scale works over a blues in the key of G. The faster you get it memorized, the faster you will be able to use it to create melodies and solos.

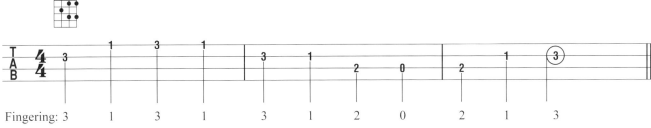

Fingering: 3   1   3   1   3   1   2   0   2   1   3

Let's cut loose a little and have some fun. Try playing the melody to Elvis Presley's classic song "Hound Dog," which mainly uses notes from the G minor pentatonic scale.

HOUND DOG

Words and Music by Jerry Leiber and Mike Stoller

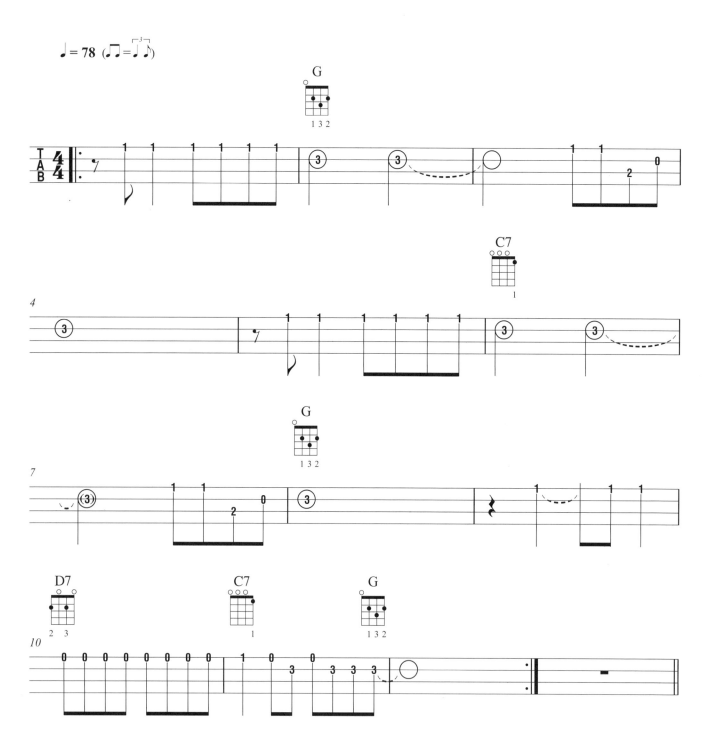

Music Reading:
3rd-String Notes

It's time to learn the two notes on the 3rd string. The C note is the 3rd string open, and the D note is on the 2nd fret of the 3rd string.

Example 1—Whole Notes

For this exercise, we'll play the C and D notes using whole notes. The note names have been written under each note to help you get started.

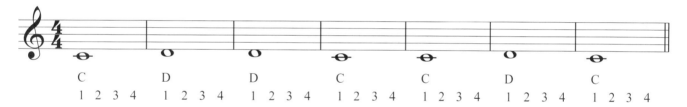

Example 2—Half Notes

This exercise uses half notes and has repeat signs.

Example 3—Quarter Notes

This exercise starts on the C note and is played with all quarter notes.

This fun little song features the C and D notes on the 3rd string. The main rhythm is a dotted quarter note (♩.), which is one-and-a-half beats, followed by an eighth note (♪), which is half of a beat.

BACKSTEP

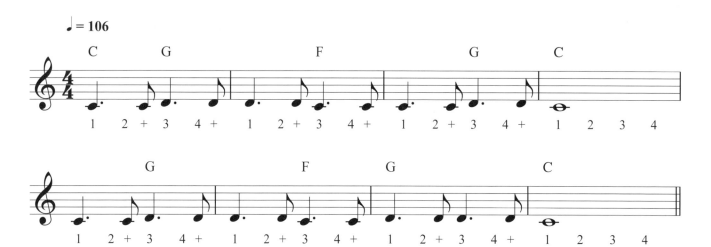

Example 4—Three-String Review

Here's a review exercise of strings 1–3 with whole notes.

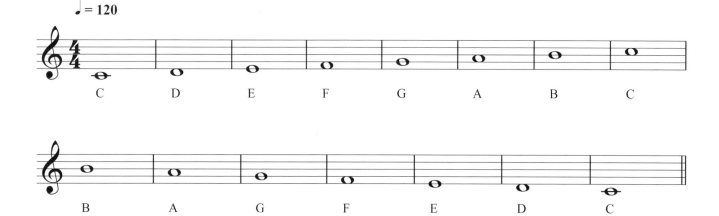

The melody for "The Wheels on the Bus" is perfect for practicing your note reading, as the notes jump around on strings 1, 2, and 3.

THE WHEELS ON THE BUS (Melody)
Traditional

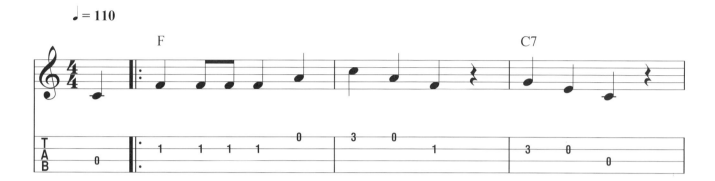

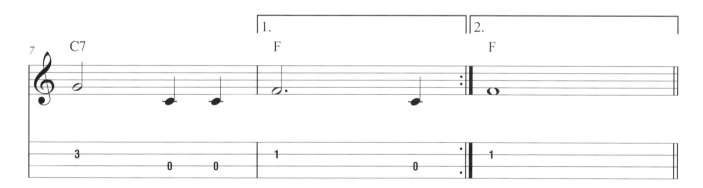

Let's use the notes from strings 1–3 to play a familiar classical piece by Ludwig van Beethoven.

ODE TO JOY
By Ludwig van Beethoven

Pro Tips & Info

Ludwig van Beethoven composed his greatest work, *Symphony No. 9*, while deaf.

Reggae

Reggae is a cool, laid-back style that originated in Jamaica. It's known for its three-note chord voicings and syncopated upstroke rhythms played on the upbeats (the "+" of each beat).

Example 1

In this example, we will just play the A chord at the 4th fret using upstrokes on all the upbeats.

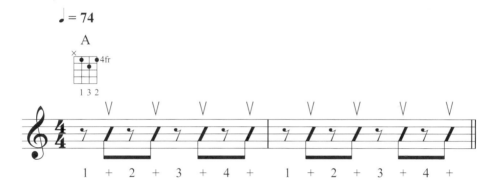

Example 2

Now, let's add the D chord at the 5th fret to give the progression a little movement.

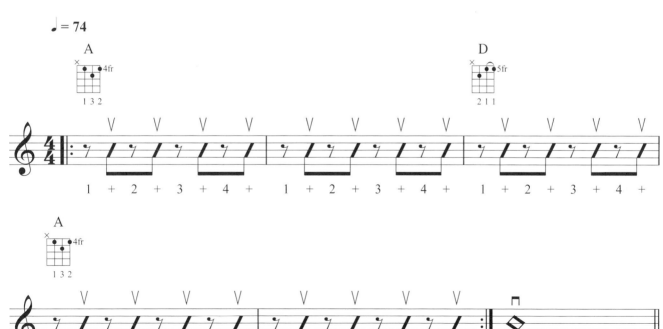

This classic progression has a reggae feel, and although it doesn't have a lot of chord changes, it is important to lock in the upstroke rhythms on the upbeats.

THREE LITTLE BIRDS
Words and Music by Bob Marley

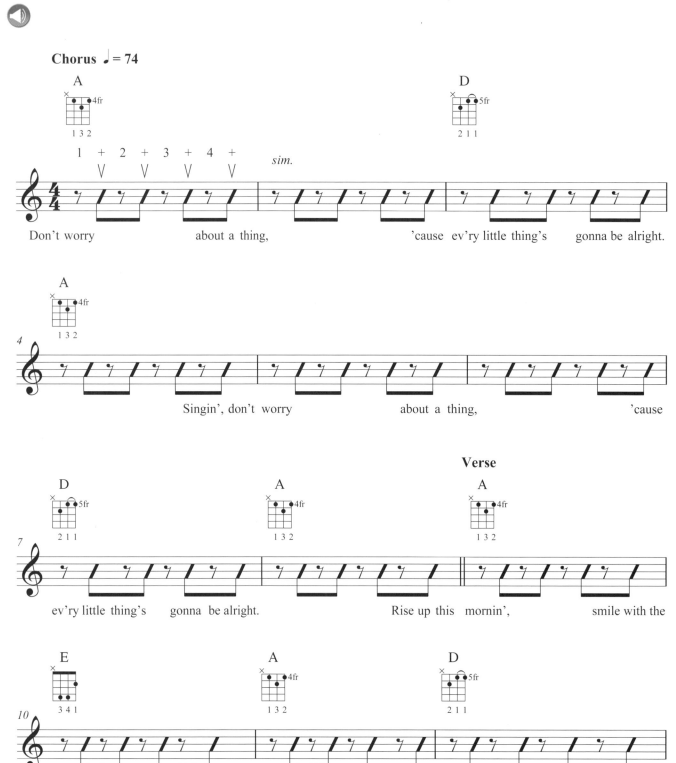

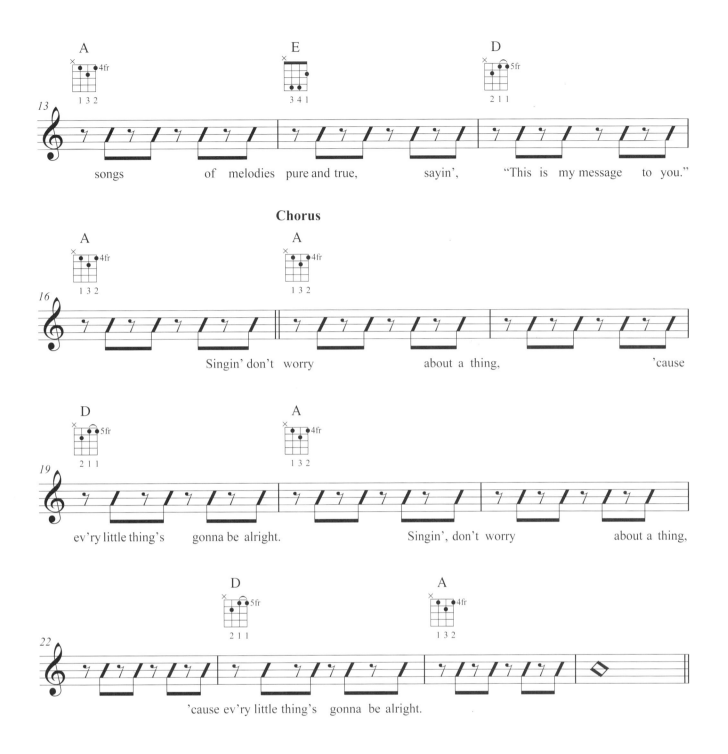

Chorus

Pro Tips & Info

Reggae music is known for its laid-back feel, three-string chord voicings, and accents on the upbeats.

Hammer-Ons and Pull-Offs
Hammer-Ons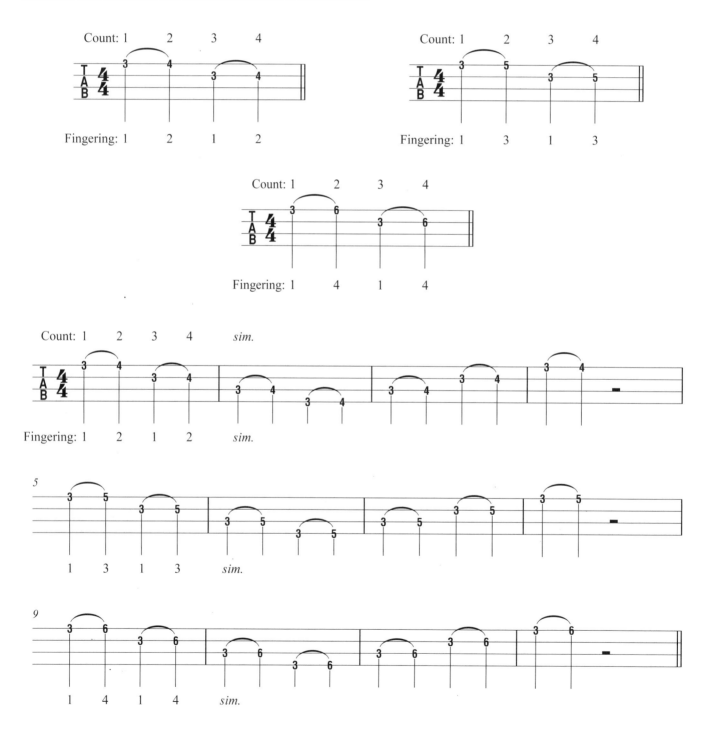

Hammer-ons are an essential fret-hand technique that can make your playing sound smoother. To hammer on, start with your 1st finger on the 1st string, 3rd fret. Pick that note, and then take your 3rd finger and "hammer" it onto the 5th fret of the 1st string. Pick only the first note at the 3rd fret; the motion of "slamming" your 3rd finger down on the 5th fret should be enough to produce a solid pitch. This will require some strength and pressure to make sure the second note is heard. Make sure to hammer on using your fingertip for good clarity and tone.

Watch the accompanying video and then practice the following hammer-on exercises. The curved line in the notation that connects the hammered notes is called a *slur*.

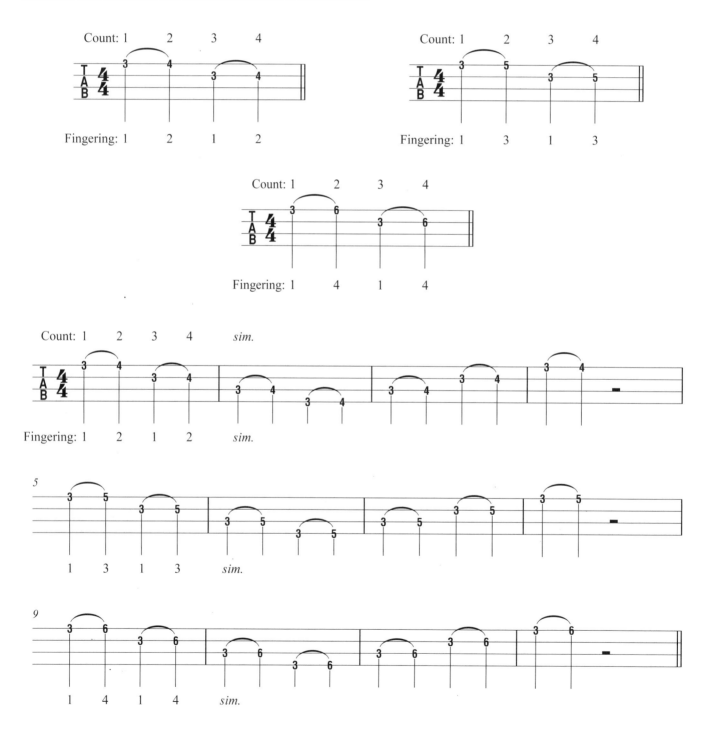

Pull-Offs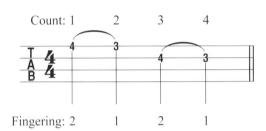

Essentially the opposite of hammer-ons, *pull-offs* are an advanced technique that will make your playing sound smoother and more professional. You can play pull-offs with all your fret-hand fingers, but typically, your 1st finger will need to be planted on the fretboard as you pull off from a higher note. For example, start with your 1st finger on the 3rd fret of the 1st string, and your 3rd finger on the 5th fret of the 1st string. Push your 3rd finger into the fretboard and then down toward the ground, letting the string snap off your finger. You will only pick the first note (5th fret), allowing the snap of the pull-off to sound the second note (3rd fret). Picking one note but hearing two notes will help your playing sound smoother.

Check out the video and then practice the following pull-off exercises. As with hammer-ons, a slur is used to connect the notes.

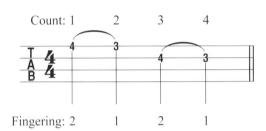

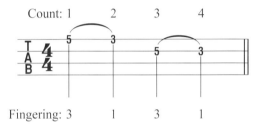

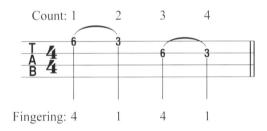

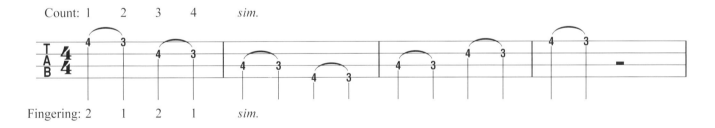

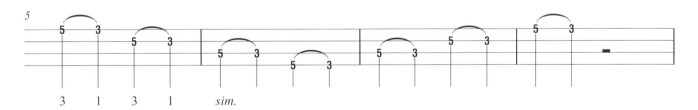

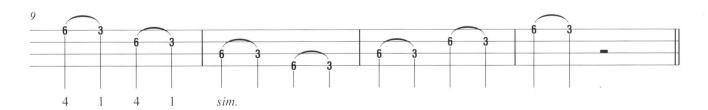

The Blues Turnaround

> **Pro Tips & Info: Grace Notes**
> A *grace note* is a small note placed in front of a main note as a musical "ornament." It has no real time value of its own but is played quickly before the main note.

Blues Turnaround in A

A *turnaround* is a short section at the end of a 12-bar blues that sets you up to go back to the beginning or to end the song. Below is one of the most iconic turnarounds you will hear, and it's used by all the blues greats. The lick starts on beat 2 and uses triplets to get its authentic sound.

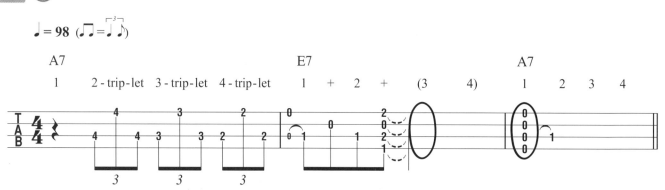

Now, let's play a boogie woogie in closed position in the key of A. A closed position does not use any open strings. This example features the turnaround we just learned.

BOOGIE WOOGIE BLUES IN A (Closed)

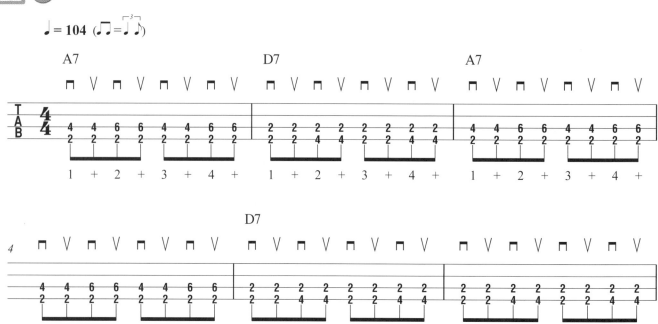

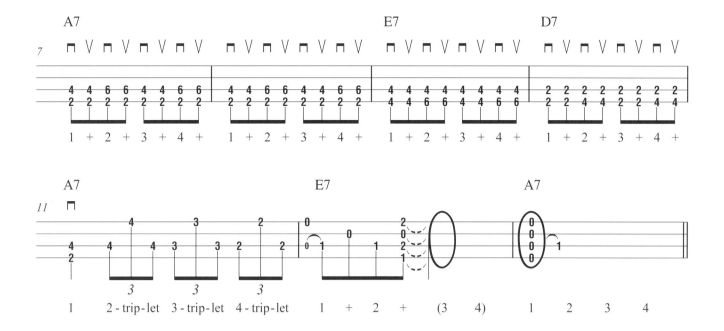

Jump Blues Solo

This example is written in the style of jump blues, which is an upbeat and lively style of blues. We'll use the C blues scale (which will be covered in more detail later) to create a shuffled riff that sounds bluesy and authentic. The chord progression is a traditional 12-bar blues in the key of C, using the I, IV, and V chords: C7, F7, and G7. The ideas you learn in this solo can be used in any blues or song in the key of C in which you want a blues sound. Work on memorizing these riffs and licks so you can use them later to create your own solos. You can play this on any ukulele tuned G-C-E-A with a high or low G. Use your thumb to play the entire tune.

BIG DOG STRUT BLUES (Solo in C)

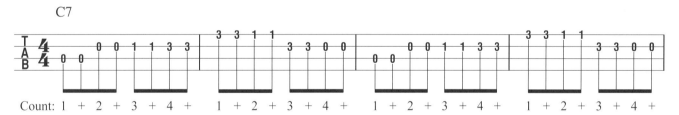

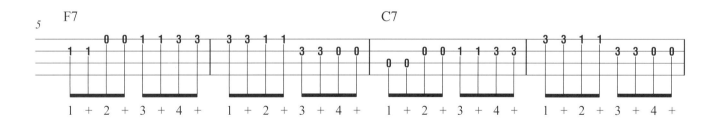

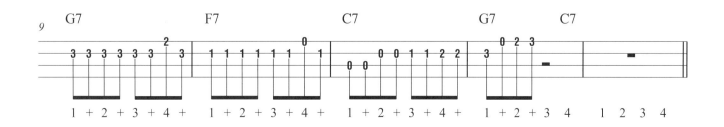

Music Reading:
High D Note

To play our next song, we need to learn the high D note, which is on the 5th fret of the 1st string. In this tune, you can play the high D with either the 3rd or 4th finger of your fretting hand.

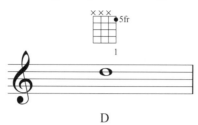

This traditional song by John Newton, written in 1800, is in 3/4 time, so there are three beats in each measure. There is a pickup note, so you will play the first note on beat 3 of your count. Additionally, there are ties across measures. In measures 7–8 and the 1st ending, a dotted half note (three beats) is tied to a half note (two beats), so you will hold the note for five beats. In the 2nd ending, a dotted quarter note is tied to another dotted quarter note, so it lasts for six beats. Remember, the first time through the song you play the 1st ending, and then after taking the repeat, you skip the 1st ending and play the 2nd ending.

AMAZING GRACE (Melody)
Words by John Newton
Traditional American Melody

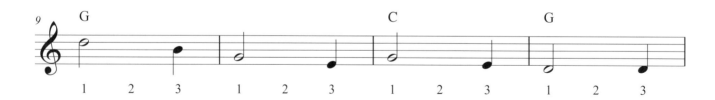

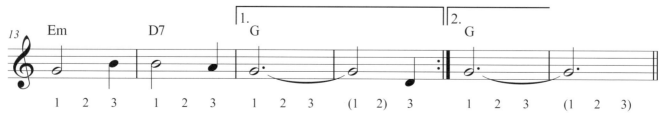

Strumming in 3/4

Now, we'll use "Amazing Grace" to try strumming in 3/4. A great pattern to start with is D D-U D-U (down, down-up, down-up). This is a downstroke quarter note on beat 1 followed by eighth notes on beats 2 and 3 that you will strum with alternating downstrokes and upstrokes.

AMAZING GRACE (Strumming)

Words by John Newton
Traditional American Melody

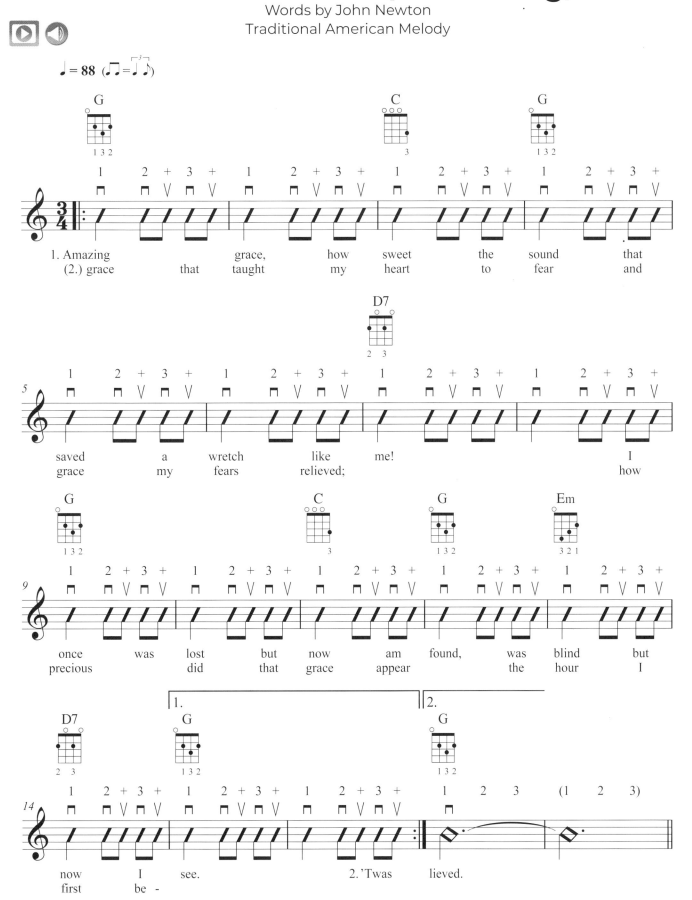

Chords:
Anticipation and Muting

Now, let's check out some new strumming concepts with more famous tunes!

The strum pattern for "La Bamba" uses a mute (x) on beat 4 and a tie on the "+" of beat 4. The G7 chord is *anticipated* because it is played on the "+" of 4, as opposed to beat 1 of the next measure.

LA BAMBA
By Richard Valenzuela

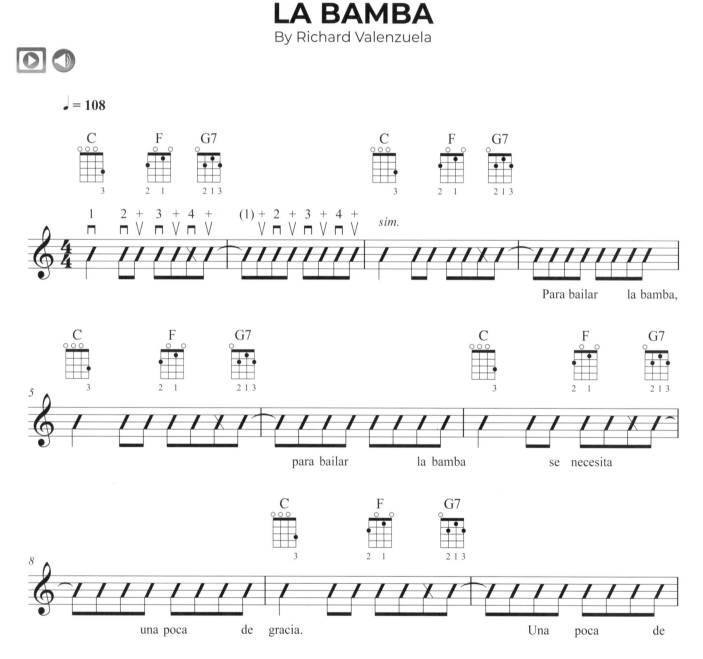

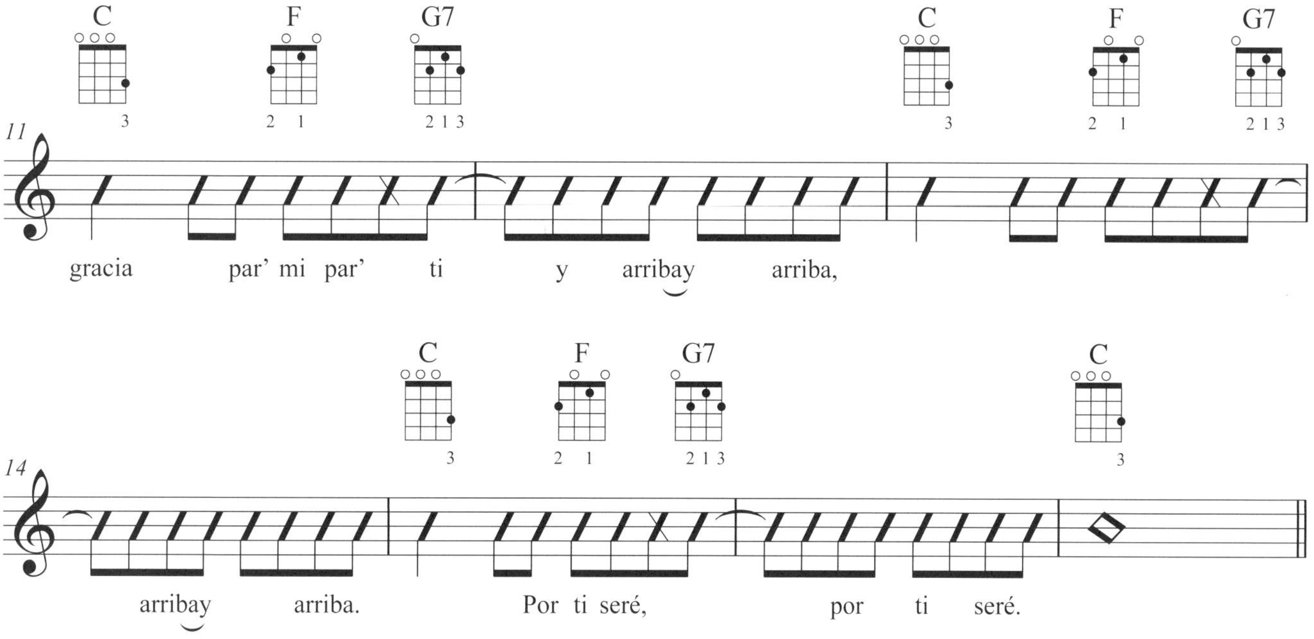
11
C F G7 C F G7
gracia par' mi par' ti y arribay arriba,
14
C F G7 C
arribay arriba. Por ti seré, por ti seré.

Pro Tips & Info

Adding a mute while strumming chords is sometimes called *chucking*, and it is indicated with an "x" in the music.

This strum pattern uses a mute (x) on beat 2 and a tie on the "+" of beat 2. The C and G chords are anticipated because they come in on the "+" of beat 2 and not on beat 3.

LEARNING TO FLY

Words and Music by Tom Petty and Jeff Lynne

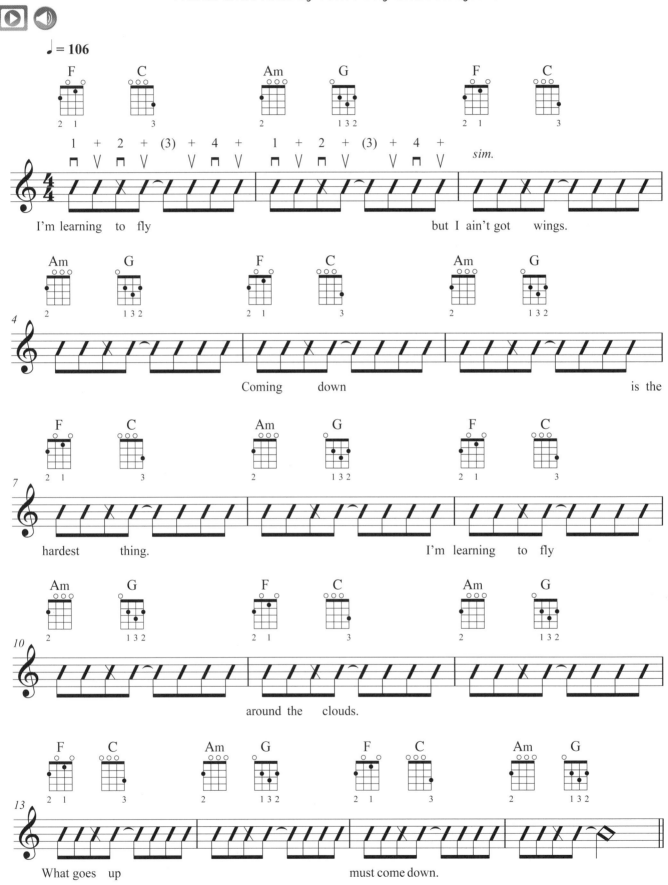

Technique Builder 3

This exercise will stretch your hands and build strength using fingers 1–4–2–3.

Fingering: 1   4   2   3   *sim.*

Fingerpicking:
p–i–m–a–m–i

This fingerpicking pattern is a *forward roll* (from low string to high) followed by a *backward roll* (from high string to low). Here, "low" and "high" refer to string numbers 4–3–2–1–2–3 that you will be plucking with the *p–i–m–a–m–i* fingerstyle pattern (thumb-index-middle-ring-middle-index).

The song we will play is in 6/8 time, which means there are six beats per measure and the eighth note gets the beat—or simply, six eighth notes per measure. In 6/8 time, the pulse is felt on the first eighth note in each three-note grouping; if you're counting 1, 2, 3, 4, 5, 6, the pulse is on beats 1 and 4.

THE HOUSE OF THE RISING SUN
Words and Music by Alan Price

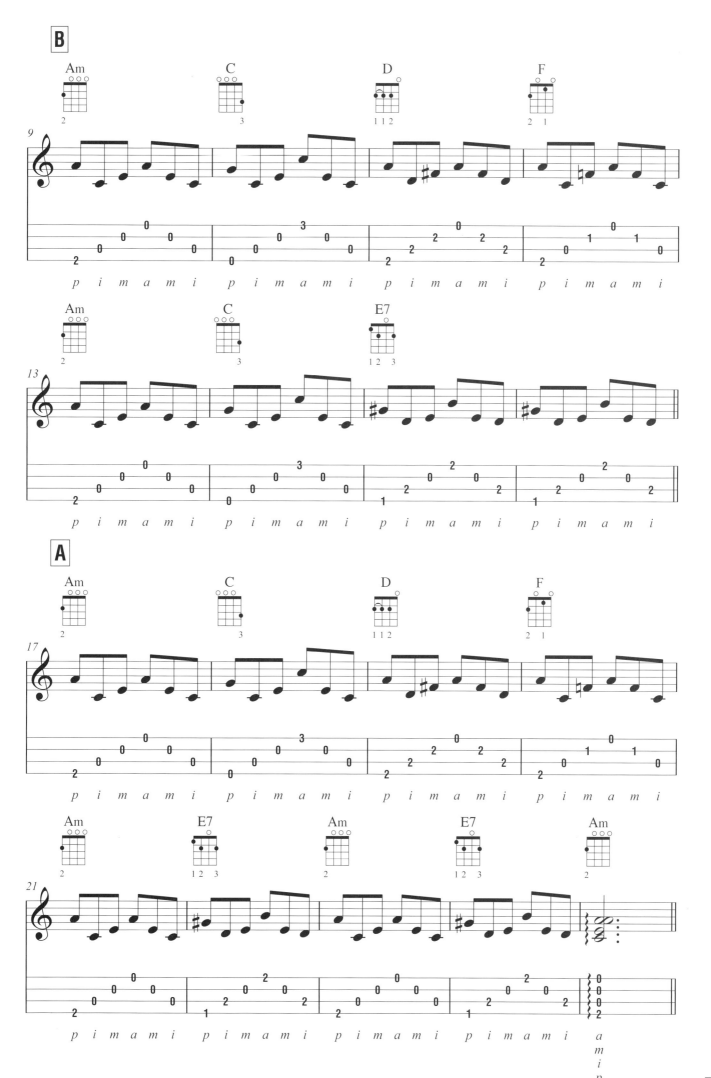

Barre Chords

Barre chords are some of the scariest chords you will learn how to play. But with a few tips and a little practice, you can do it. There are two types of barre chords: the partial barre chord and the full barre chord. The partial barre chord, such as the B♭ chord, is when your barring finger, usually your index, covers two strings. A full barre chord, like the C7 chord, is when your barring finger covers all four strings of the ukulele.

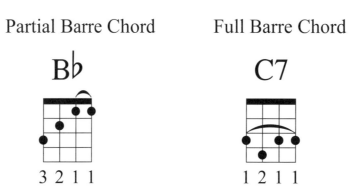

Here are three tips to help you play your barre chords smoothly and clearly:

1. Make sure your index barring finger is parallel to the frets. You do not want your index finger to be slanted at an angle compared to the fret.

2. Move your barre right up next to the fret but not on top of the fret. You will not be able to get clear notes if you barre on top of the fret.

3. Be sure to apply adequate pressure on each string to get a clear tone.

C Minor Blues

This slow minor blues uses the Cm7, Fm, Ab7, G7, and G7+ chords. The G7+ is an augmented 7th chord, and the Cm7 is a full barre chord. The rhythm is made up of eighth notes with mutes on beats 2 and 4 and a tie from the "+" of beat 2 to beat 3.

THE THRILL IS GONE
Words and Music by Roy Hawkins and Rick Darnell

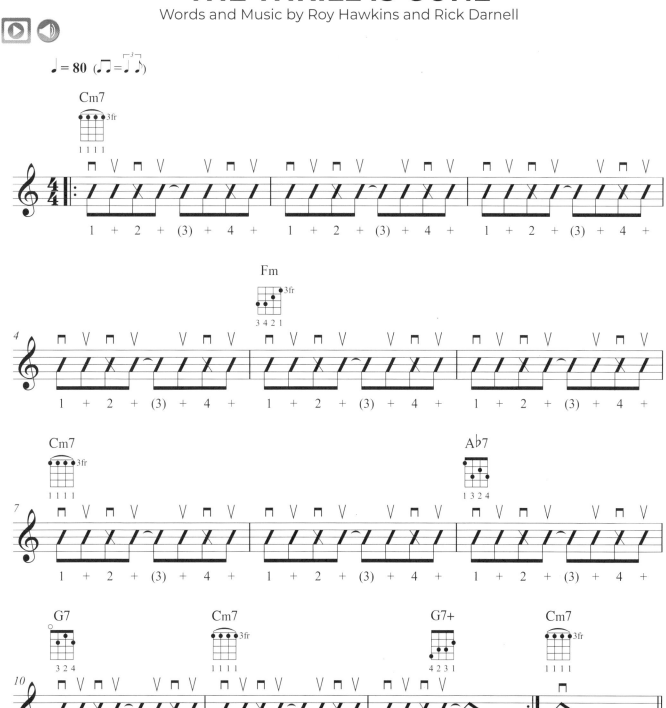

C Minor Pentatonic Scale (Open)

The C minor pentatonic scale is perfect for soloing over a blues or rock song in the key of C.

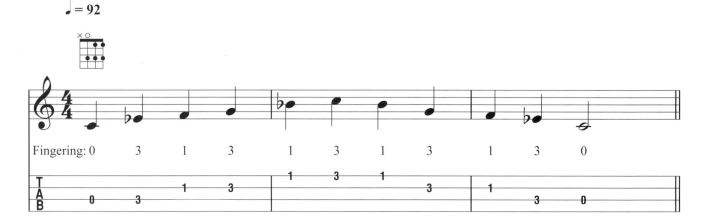

C Blues Scale (Open)

As mentioned in a previous lesson, the blues scale is essentially the same as the minor pentatonic scale, but it has one extra note—the ♭5, or G♭ in the key of C.

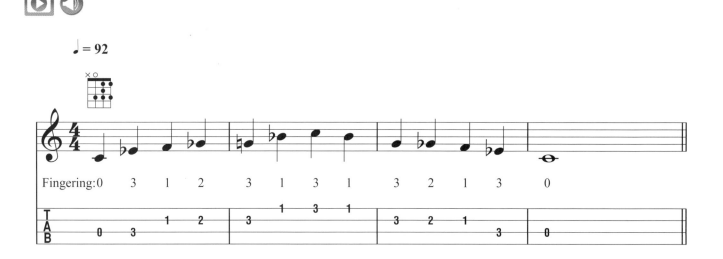

Memorize both scales and then try the solo that follows.

The solo on the next page is based on the C blues scale, and we'll play it over the minor blues chord progression from "The Thrill Is Gone." However, you can use the licks and ideas in this solo over any blues or song in the key of C when you're looking for a blues sound. You can play this on any ukulele tuned G-C-E-A, with a high or low G string. Use your thumb to play the entire solo.

BLUES ETUDE (Solo in C)

♩ = 80

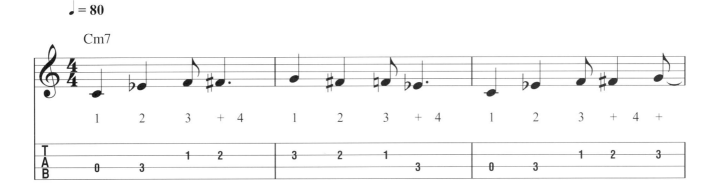

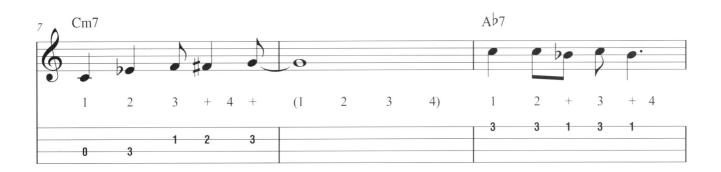

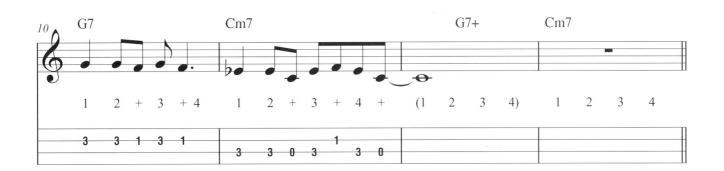

Pro Tips & Info

Having trouble playing? Consider having a luthier do a setup on your uke to lower the strings. This will bring them closer to the fretboard and make them easier to press down.

Music Reading:
High E and F Notes

To play the next song, we'll need to look at two new notes. We already learned the D note, which is on the 5th fret of the 1st string. Now, we'll look at the E note, which is on the 7th fret of the 1st string, and the F note, which is on the 8th fret of the 1st string.

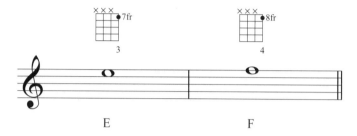

"Aura Lee" is an American Civil War song written by W.W. Fosdick and George R. Poulton. Elvis Presley adapted this melody in his song "Love Me Tender." The song's rhythm is pretty simple, but we'll be using the high D, E, and F notes. In addition, you can play the A note on the open 1st string, or you can try playing it on the 5th fret of the 2nd string.

AURA LEE
Words by W.W. Fosdick
Music by George R. Poulton

Sixteenth-Note Rhythms

Sixteenth notes get one-fourth of a beat, so you can have four sixteenth notes per beat. Sixteenth notes are counted:

1 e + a, 2 e + a, 3 e + a, 4 e + a

Here's a review of all the note types, with the addition of the sixteenth note:

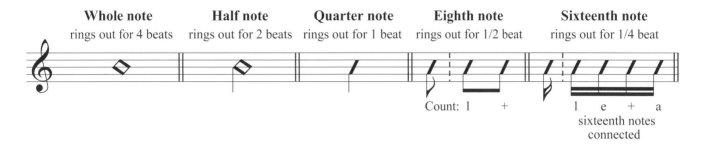

Let's try some sixteenth-note rhythms mixed in with whole notes, half notes, quarter notes, and eighth notes. We'll play these rhythms using a C chord.

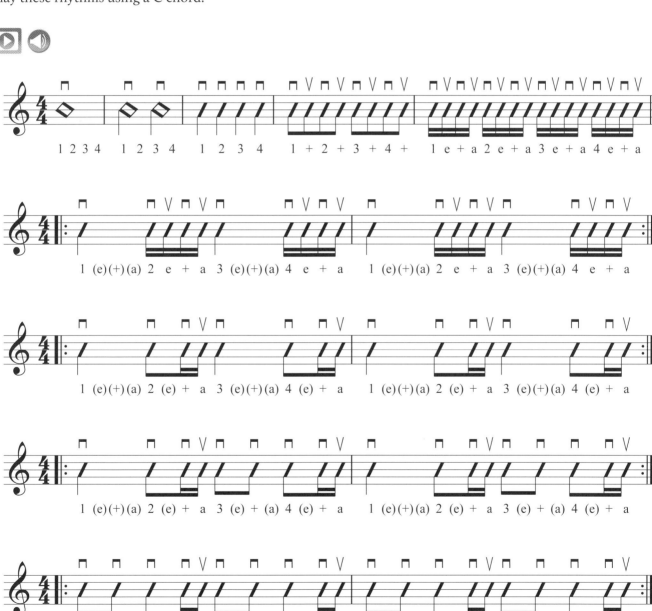

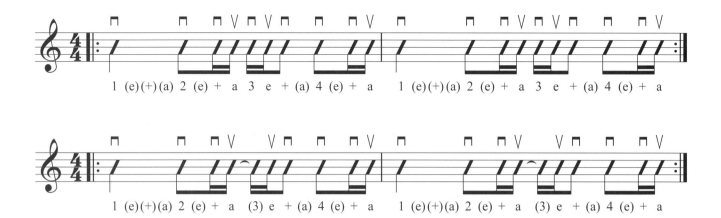

Let's revisit the chord progression for "Let It Be," but this time we are going to strum using sixteenth notes. The sixteenth-note rhythms on beats 2 and 4 will add some activity to the strumming and lift up the song.

LET IT BE
Words and Music by John Lennon and Paul McCartney

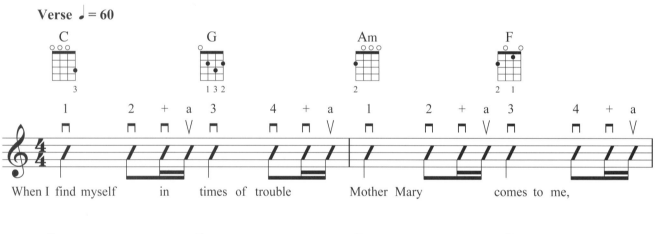

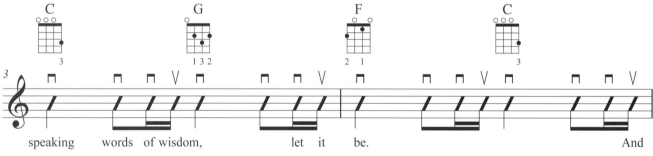

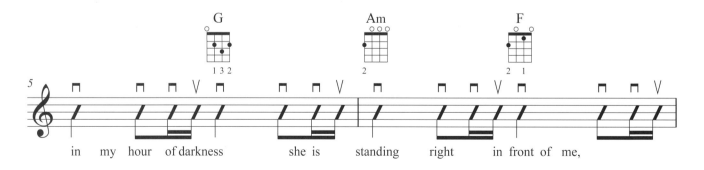

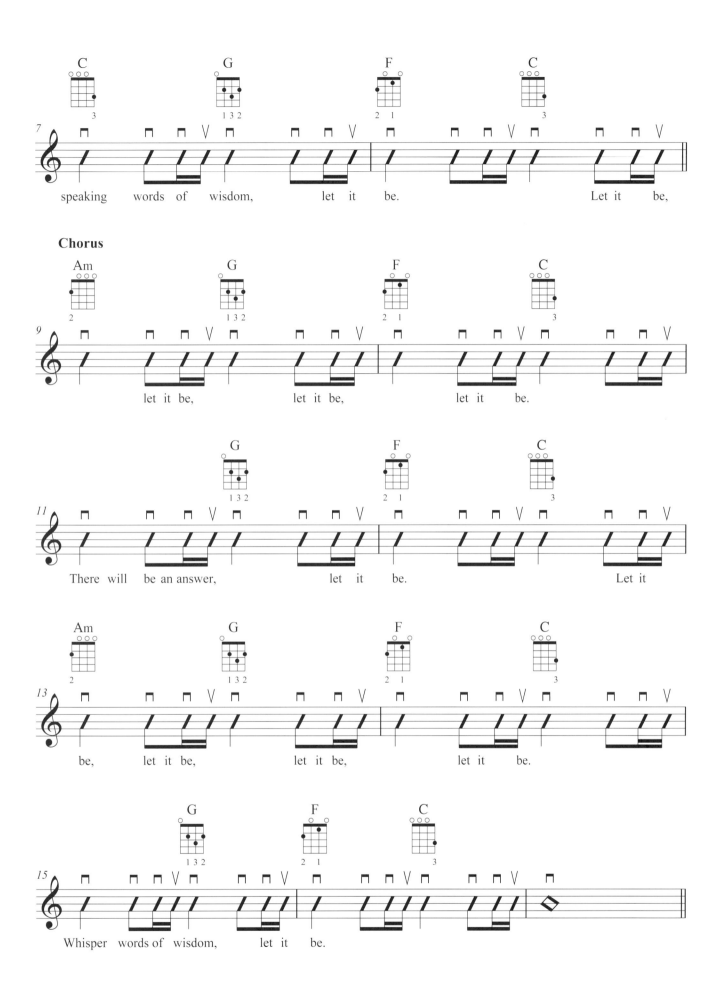

Here, we have a contemporary chord progression with another sixteenth-note strum pattern. We also have a new chord: the B♭ barre chord.

OLD TOWN ROAD
(I GOT THE HORSES IN THE BACK)

Words and Music by Trent Reznor, Atticus Ross, Kiowa Roukema and Montero Lamar Hill

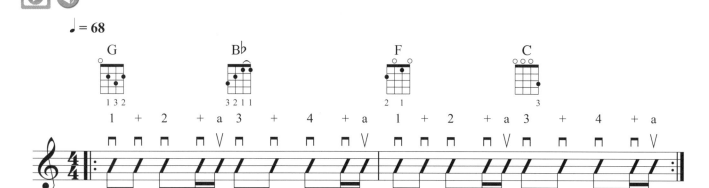

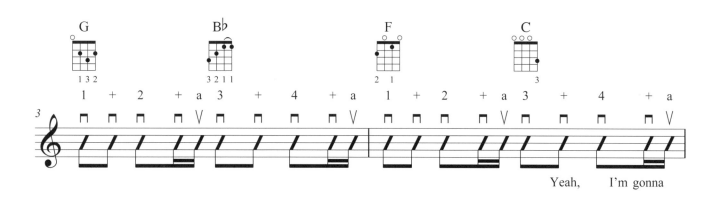

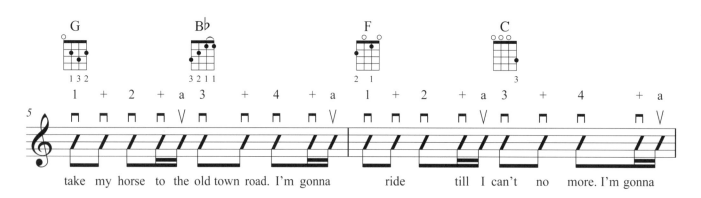

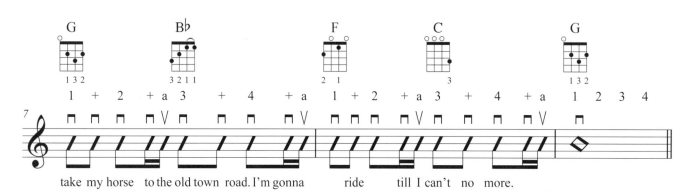

Fingerpicking:
The Pinch

This next tune features a *pinch* with *p* (thumb) and *a* (ring finger) on strings 1 and 4, followed by a pluck with the *i* (index) and *m* (middle) fingers on strings 2 and 3. The chord diagrams show the exact chord shapes for your fretting hand.

This song also features a *drone*, or *pedal tone*—a note that is held constant throughout a series of chords. In "Red Flash," the open G string is used for every chord.

At the end, there is a ritardando (*rit.*); remember, this tells you to gradually slow down the tempo.

RED FLASH

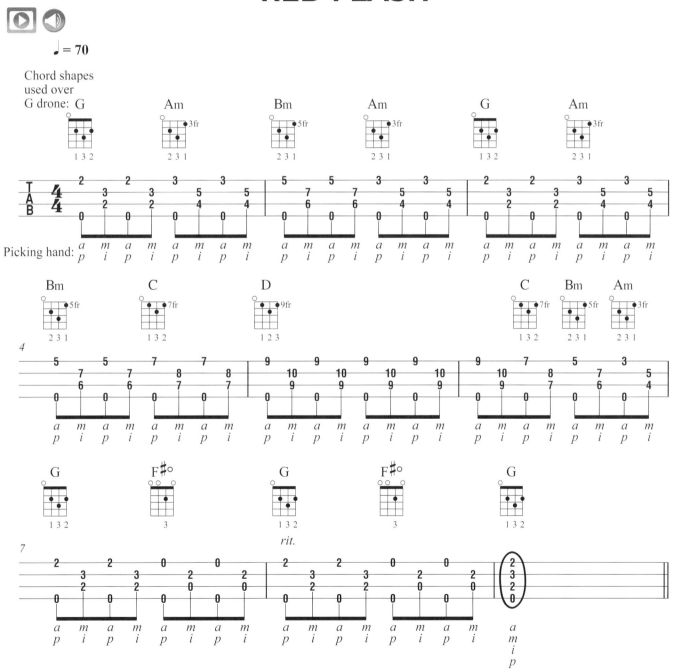

Pro Tips & Info

Change your strings when your ukulele sounds dull, the strings are fraying, or they aren't staying in tune like they used to.

Must-Know Ukulele Song No. 1

This simple three-chord progression may be one of the most recognizable songs in ukulele history—"Riptide" by Vance Joy. We are going to use a contemporary sixteenth-note strum pattern with ties on the "+" of beats 1 and 3, which means you will not strum on the downbeat of beats 2 and 4.

RIPTIDE

Words and Music by Vance Joy

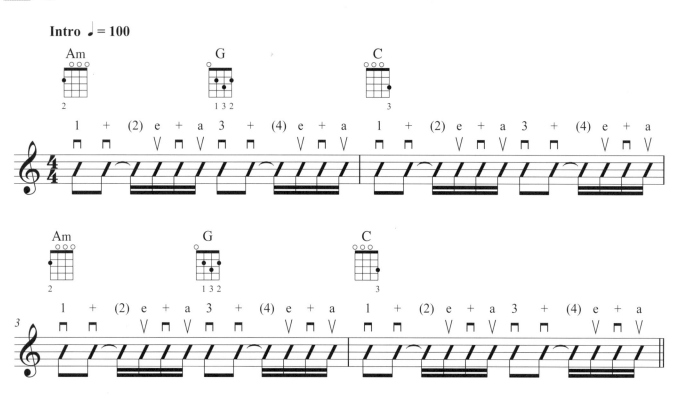

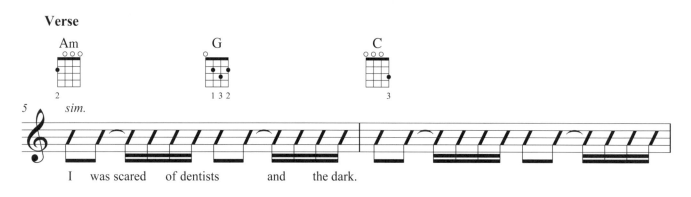

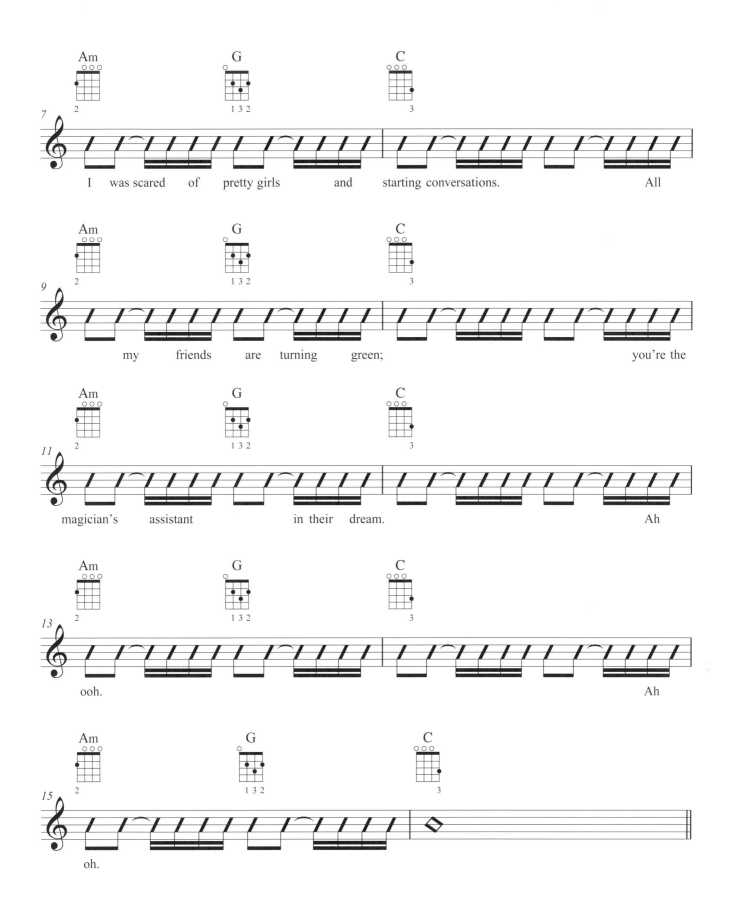

Must-Know Ukulele Song No. 2

This is essentially the same chord progression as "Let It Be," but when you add this super cool strum pattern with mutes, you get the sound and feel of "I'm Yours" by Jason Mraz. On beats 1 and 3, you will use your strumming hand to mute the strings, but you will also release pressure on the chords with your fretting hand so that you are just touching the strings but not pressing them against the fretboard. This will take some practice, but it will give you the proper sound for these mutes.

I'M YOURS
Words and Music by Jason Mraz

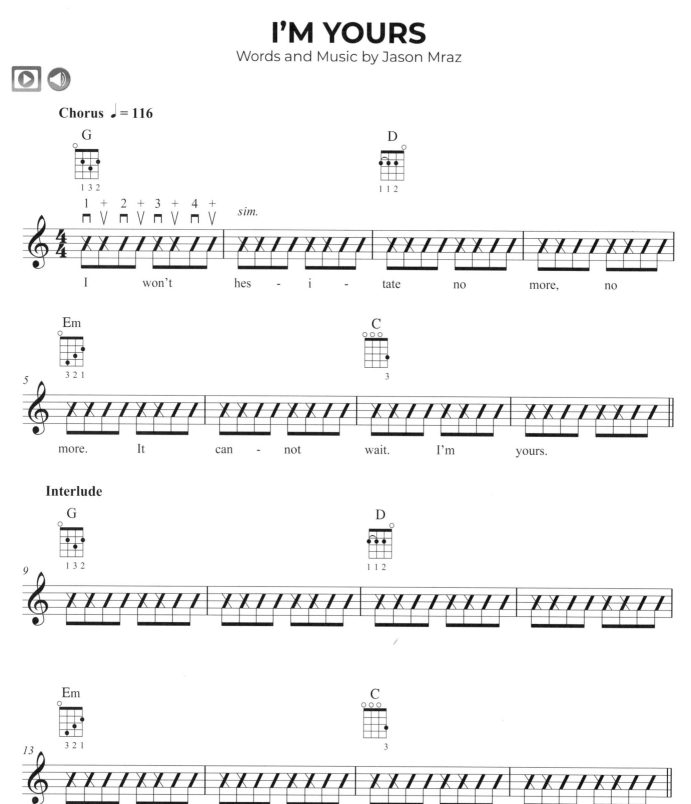

Verse

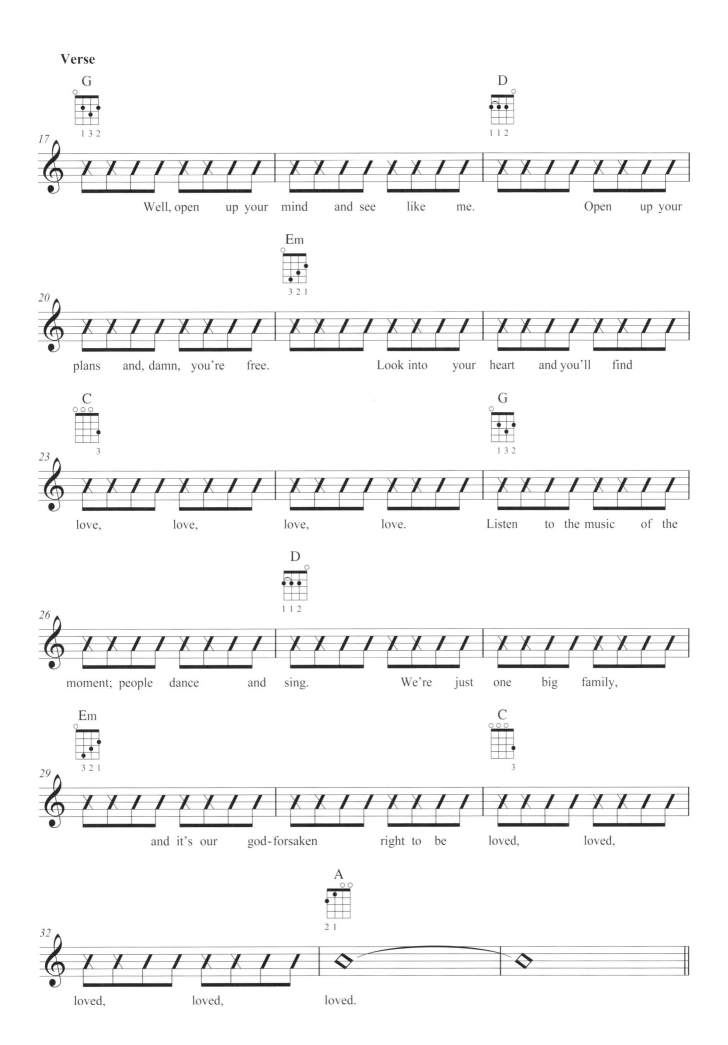

Must-Know Ukulele Song No. 3

This is one of the most challenging songs to play in the entire book as it features a complex sixteenth-note strum pattern and also some difficult ukulele chords. Although you could play this in an easier key, sometimes you have to step out of your comfort zone so your skills can increase. The strum pattern is almost entirely sixteenth notes, which gives it a driving and funky sound, and there are several barre chords.

HEY, SOUL SISTER

Words and Music by Pat Monahan, Espen Lind and Amund Bjorklund

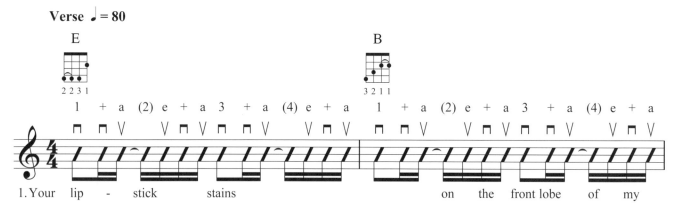

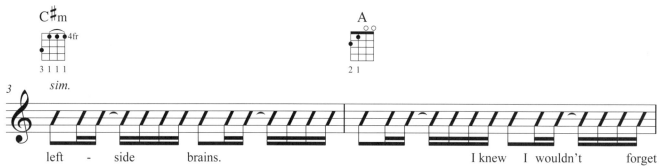

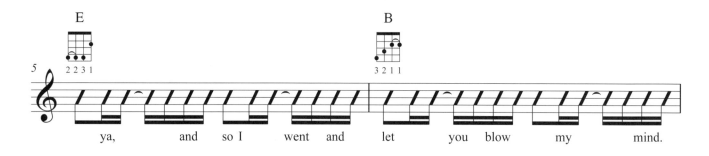

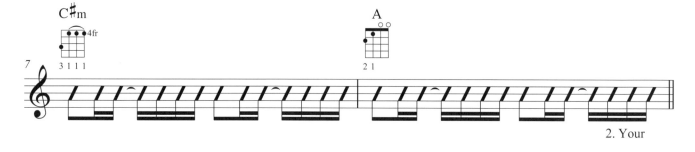

Verse

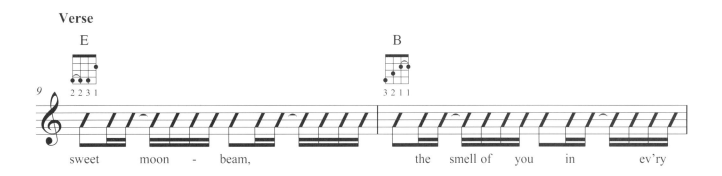

sweet   moon - beam,   the smell of you in ev'ry

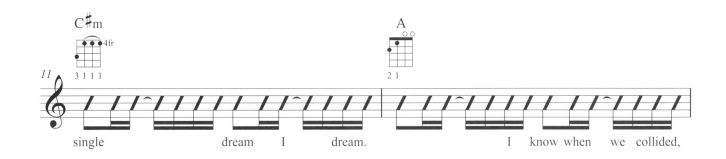

single   dream I   dream.   I know when we collided,

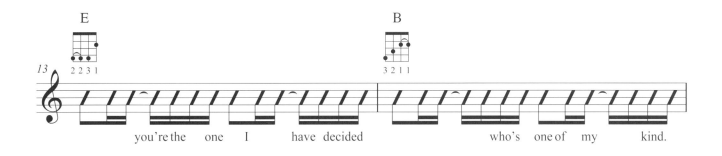

you're the one I have decided   who's one of my   kind.

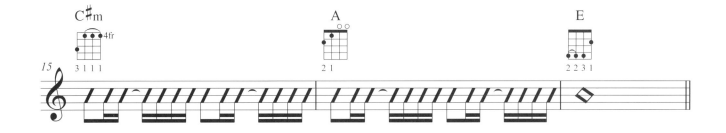

Pro Tips & Info

Joining a local ukulele group or an online community such as **Uke Like the Pros** will allow you to experience ukulele with others, which makes playing even more enjoyable.

Song in 6/8

We've already played a fingerstyle piece in 6/8 time ("The House of the Rising Sun"); now, we'll work on strumming in 6/8. We'll strum using all downstrokes, and to add variety to the pattern, don't forget to accent beats 1 and 4. As indicated by the tempo mark, the pulse of this song is on the dotted quarter note—even though there are still six eighth-note beats per measure.

HALLELUJAH
Words and Music by Leonard Cohen

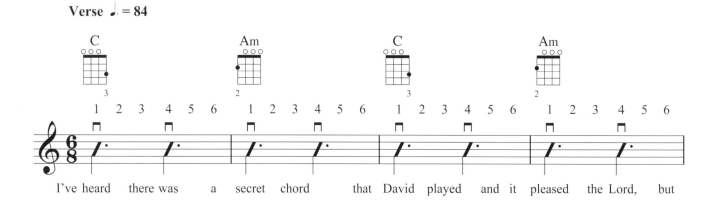

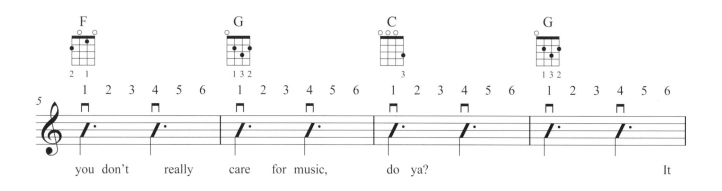

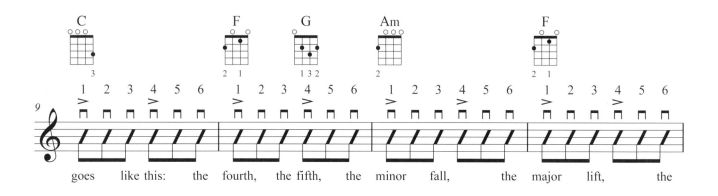

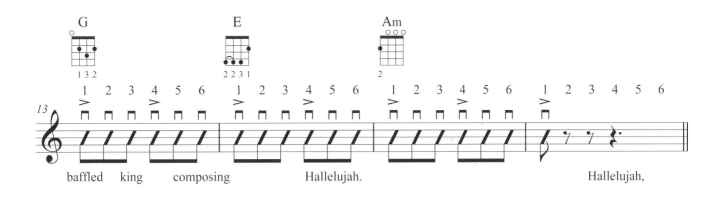

baffled   king   composing   Hallelujah.   Hallelujah,

Chorus

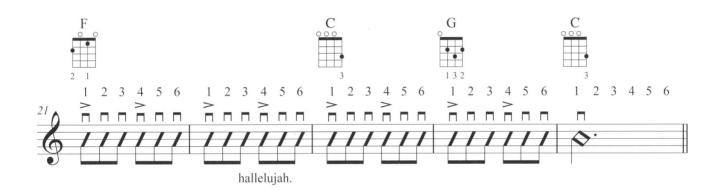

hallelujah,   hallelujah,

hallelujah.

Song in 12/8

Taking the 6/8 idea further, we'll play a standard chord progression, G–Em–C–D, and give it a 12/8 feel. The 12/8 time signature is used a lot in pop and blues songs. In 12/8, there are 12 eighth notes per measure instead of the six eighth notes in 6/8.

For this song, start with 12 downstrokes per measure. Then, you can loosen up the rhythm once you are comfortable with the 12/8 feel.

PERFECT
Words and Music by Ed Sheeran

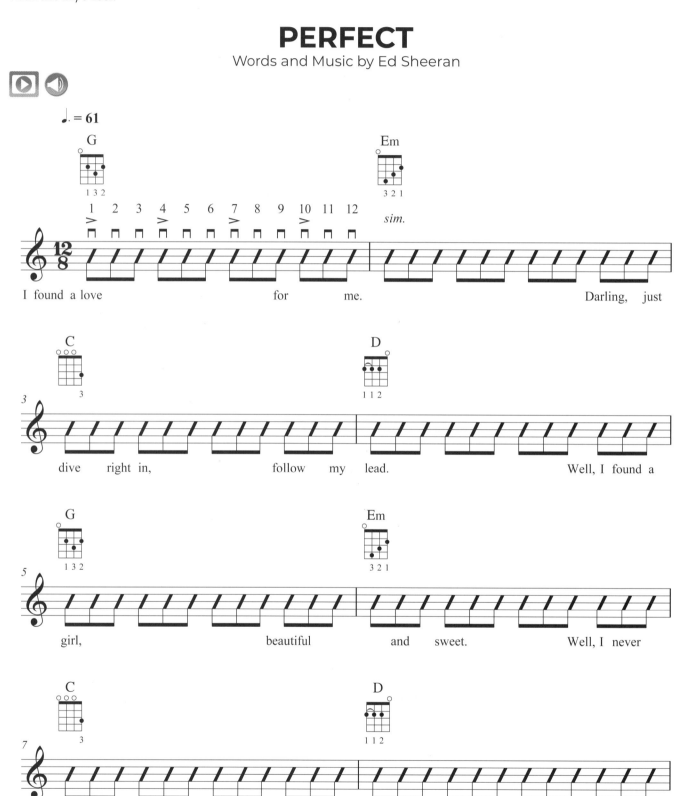

Strumming and Fingerpicking Elvis

This popular ukulele song was originally recorded by Elvis Presley and then more recently by the band Twenty One Pilots. Either way, it's a fun and fairly simple progression using a down-up eighth-note strum for the entire song.

CAN'T HELP FALLING IN LOVE (Strumming)

Words and Music by George David Weiss, Hugo Peretti and Luigi Creatore

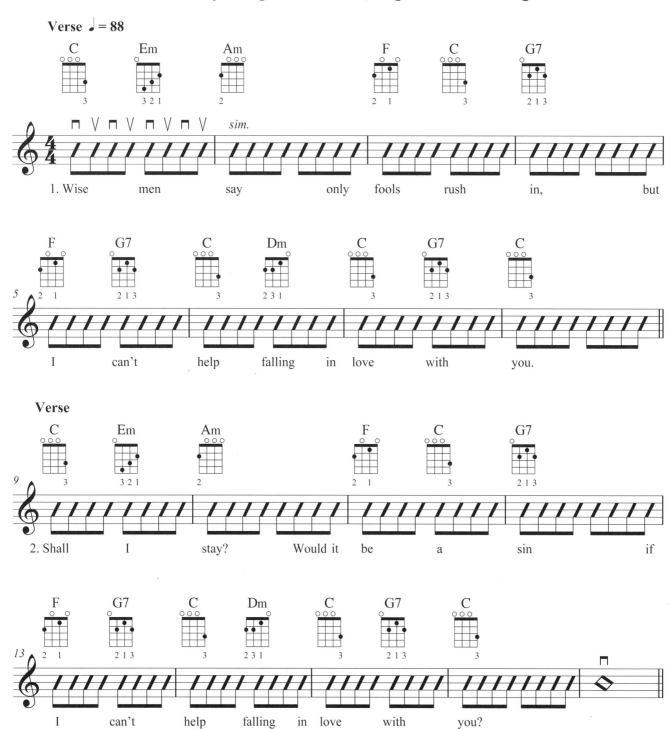

Now, we're going to play the same chord progression fingerstyle instead of strumming it. We'll use the *p–i–m–a* pattern for this one. Remember, that's thumb (*p*), index (*i*), middle (*m*), and ring (*a*). This is one of the most important fingerstyle patterns to know.

CAN'T HELP FALLING IN LOVE (Fingerstyle)

Words and Music by George David Weiss, Hugo Peretti and Luigi Creatore

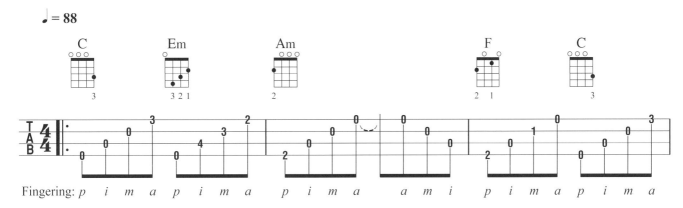

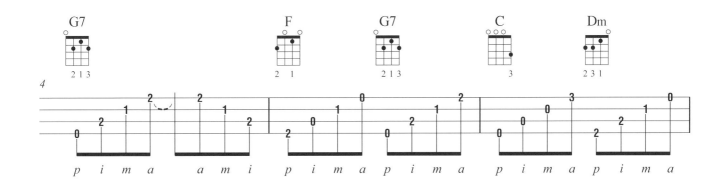

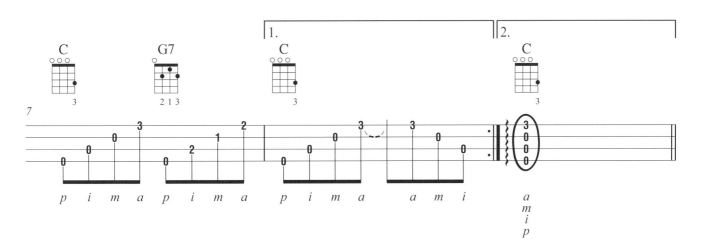

Jazz Blues

The biggest difference between a jazz blues and a traditional blues is the addition of more chords (such as the B♭7 and F7), and the *four-to-the-floor* strum pattern (four quarter-note downstrokes per measure with accents on beats 2 and 4).

JAZZ BLUES IN A

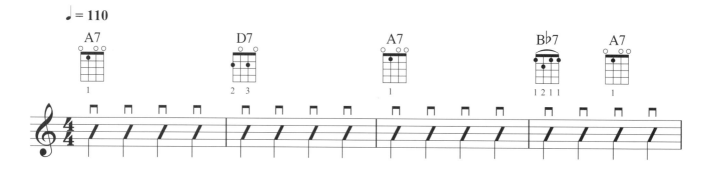

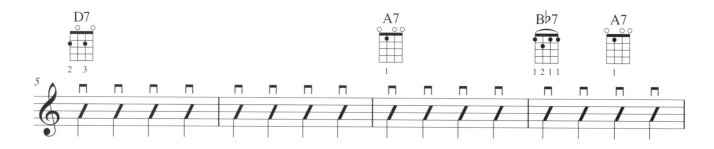

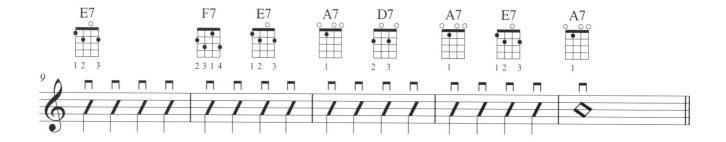

Pro Tips & Info

To get an authentic jazz sound, accent (play slightly louder on) beats 2 and 4.

Riffs and Intros

Let's check out a few fun, familiar riffs and intros from famous songs! You'll encounter some challenging new rhythms and concepts here. Each example is presented in both standard notation and tablature.

This mega hit song by the White Stripes uses strings 1–3. Notice the *quarter-note triplet* rhythms. This is similar to an eighth-note triplet, but instead of dividing a quarter note into three equal parts, it divides a *half note* into three equal parts.

SEVEN NATION ARMY
Words and Music by Jack White

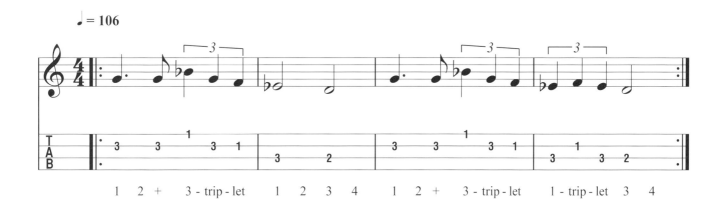

This super cool intro lick to Van Morrison's "Brown Eyed Girl" uses two-note chords called *dyads*. The notes are played together with the fingerpicking pinch technique. This intro sounds great with either a high or low G string. Both versions are notated so you can see the difference. You can also hear the difference with the two provided demonstration audio tracks.

BROWN EYED GIRL
Words and Music by Van Morrison

 *High G Version*

High G-String Version

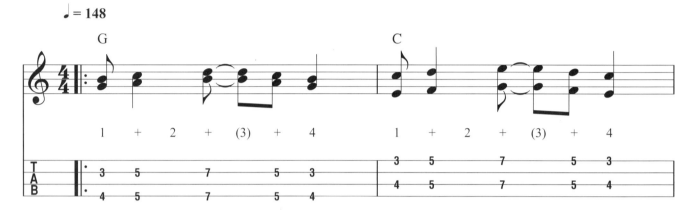

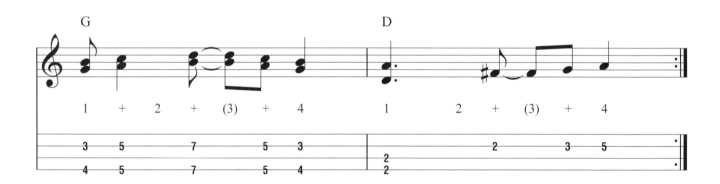

Low G Version

Low G-String Version

♩ = 148

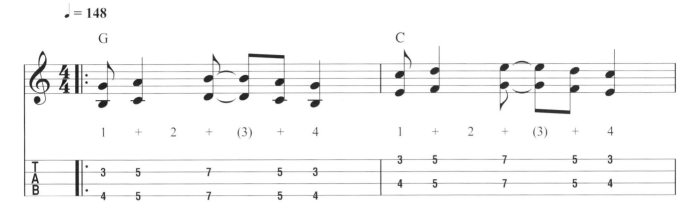

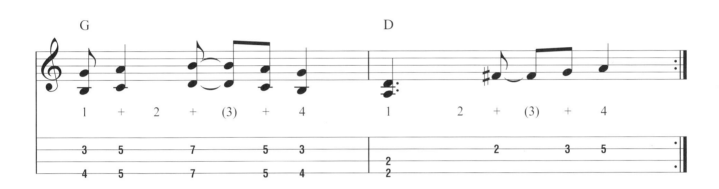

Here's the intro to "La Bamba" played in a high register and position on the neck. As you can see, many notes can be played in more than one location on the ukulele (for example, the first G note played on the 7th fret of the 3rd string).

LA BAMBA
By Richard Valenzuela

 *High G Version*

High G-String Version

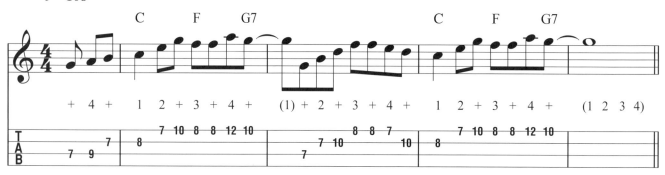

 Low G Version

Low G-String Version

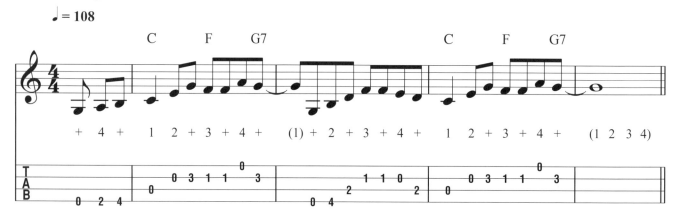

Moveable Chords

The concept of *moveable chords* is one of the most useful tools to grasp on the ukulele. By knowing just a few *closed-position* chord shapes (chords that contain no open strings), you'll be able to quickly find any chord you need, allowing you to play songs in *any* key!

The following pages will guide you through seven common moveable chord shapes, with accompanying video tutorials and notation. Understanding moveable chords not only opens the door to quickly learning hundreds of new chords, it also helps you learn the notes of the ukulele fretboard!

Moveable C Chord

The C chord is the first chord that most players learn. If you move the C chord up the neck, it will open up a new world of chords, like C♯ (or D♭). The trick to moving the C chord up the neck is that you have to move the entire shape up the fretboard, including the open strings. The C chord is **0-0-0-3** (**0** = open, **3** = 3rd fret); in other words, it is played with the open 4th, 3rd, and 2nd strings, and with the 3rd fret of the 1st string. If you move the entire shape up one fret to the C♯/D♭ chord, then you're fingering **1-1-1-4** (**1** = 1st fret, **4** = 4th fret), which is the 1st fret of the 4th, 3rd, and 2nd strings, plus the 4th fret of the 1st string. It is easiest to barre all four of the strings at the 1st fret and then use the pinky to fret the 1st string at the 4th fret. You can continue moving this shape up the neck to play the chords D, D♯/E♭, E, F, and more.

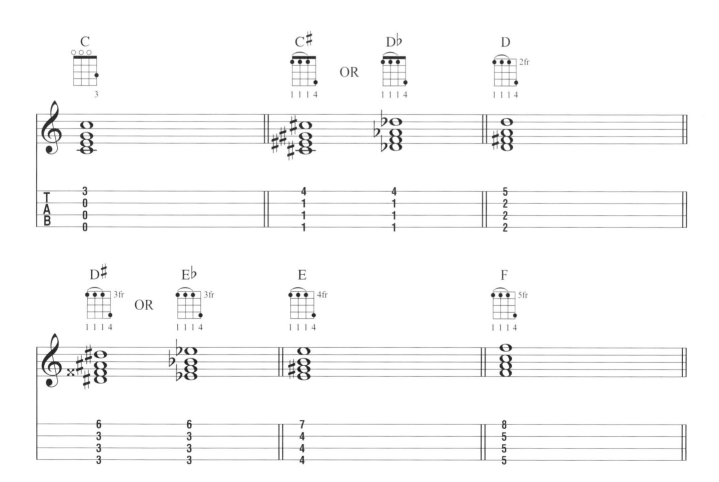

Moveable G7 Chord

Learning to move the G7 chord up the fretboard will be great when trying to play the more challenging chords like G#7 or Ab7. When you move the entire G7 shape up one fret to G#7/Ab7, you will have to re-finger the new chord to free up your 1st finger for the 4th string. You can continue to move the shape up the fretboard to A7, A#7/Bb7, B7, C7, and more.

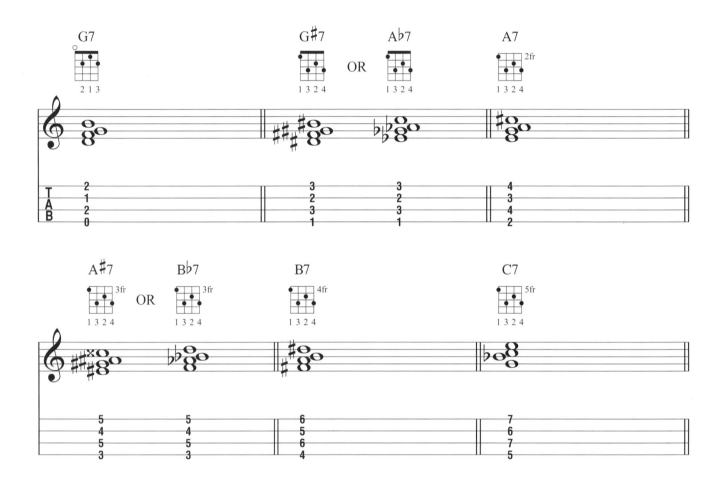

Moveable Am Chord

It's hard to play many minor chords with only open strings. Taking the Am chord shape and moving it up the fretboard will give you many hard-to-find minor chords. When you move the Am chord up one fret to the 1st fret, you will get the A♯m/B♭m chord. To make it easier, barre strings 1–3 with your index finger, and use your 3rd finger on the 4th string, 3rd fret. When you continue to move the shape up, you get Bm, Cm, C♯m/D♭m, Dm, and more.

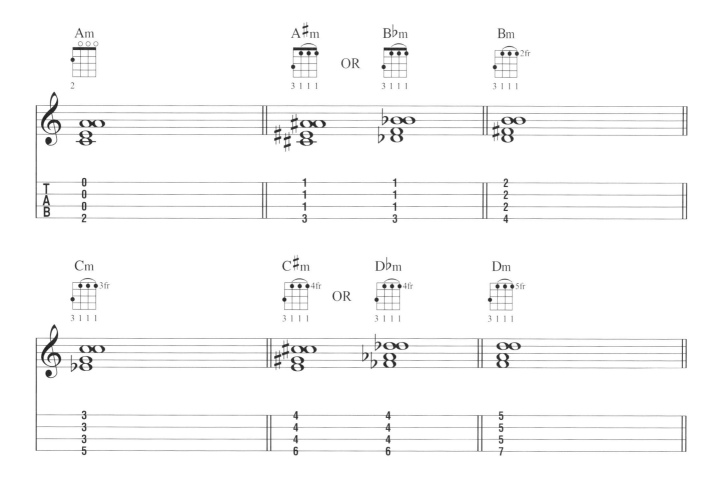

Moveable F Chord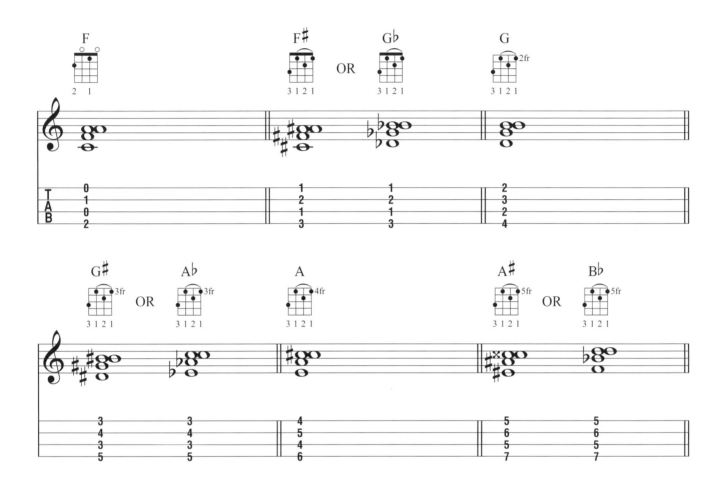

The F chord is one of the most common chords you will play. When you move the shape up to the 1st fret, you get the F#/Gb chord. The new fingering for this chord will be to barre strings 1–3 with your index finger, with the 2nd finger on the 2nd string, 2nd fret, and the 3rd finger on the 4th string, 3rd fret. Keep this same fingering as you move up the fretboard to play the chords G, G#/Ab, A, A#/Bb, B, C, and more.

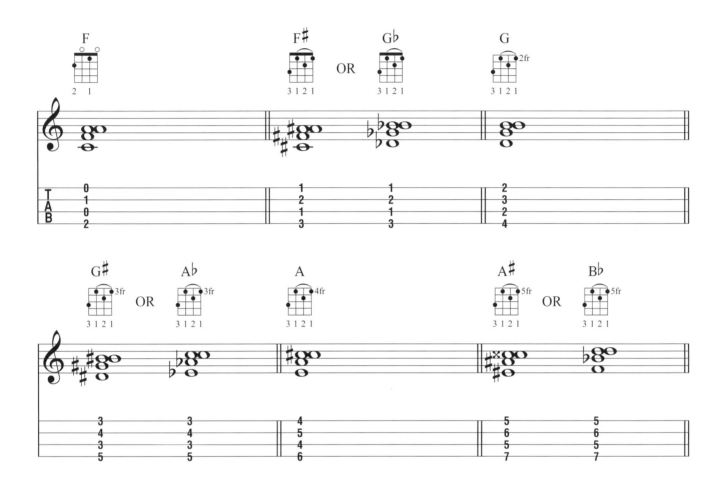

Moveable D Chord

The D chord is one of the most difficult shapes to play on the ukulele. There are several different fingerings you can use to fret the D chord. Regardless of the fingering you choose, you will have to re-finger the chord once you move it up the neck. When you move the chord to the 1st fret—to the D♯/E♭ chord—place your 1st finger on the 1st string, 1st fret, and use your 2nd finger to barre the 3rd/4th strings at the 3rd fret; use your 3rd finger on the 2nd string, 3rd fret. Even this fingering can be adjusted to what works for your hand. As you move up the fretboard, you will get the chords E, F, F♯/G♭, G, and more.

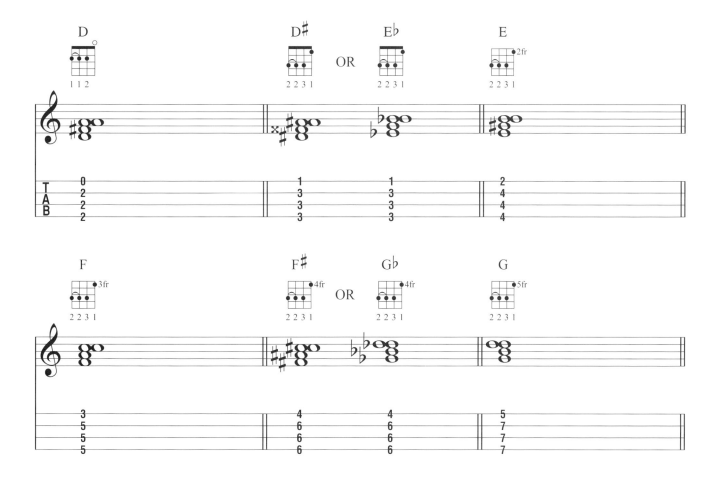

Moveable Dm Chord

Dm is a cool-sounding chord that isn't too hard to play. When you move the shape up one fret to the D♯m/E♭m chord, change your fingering by using the 1st finger on the 1st string, 1st fret; 2nd finger on the 2nd string, 2nd fret; 3rd finger on the 4th string, 3rd fret; and 4th finger to the 3rd string, 3rd fret. As you move the shape up the neck, you will play the chords Em, Fm, F♯m/G♭m, Gm, and more.

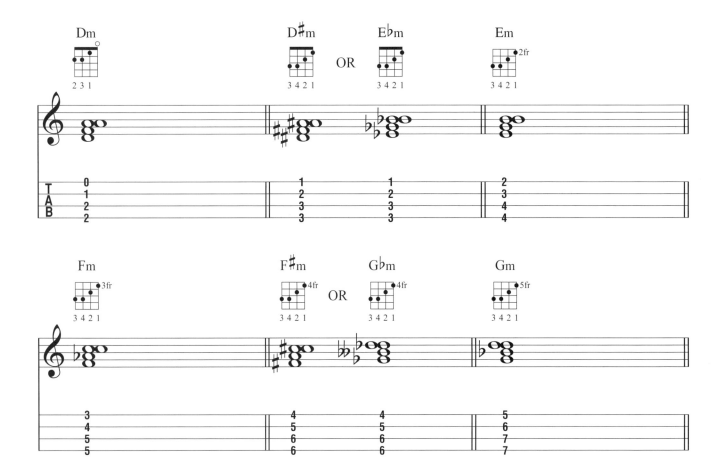

Moveable A Chord

The A chord shape will be one of the most valuable shapes to know for moving around the neck. When you move it up to the 1st fret, you are playing the A#/B♭ chord. Re-finger the chord so your 1st finger barres the 1st and 2nd strings at the 1st fret. Use your 2nd finger on the 3rd string, 2nd fret, and your 3rd finger on the 4th string, 3rd fret. As you move this great shape up the neck, you'll find chords like B, C, C#/D♭, and D.

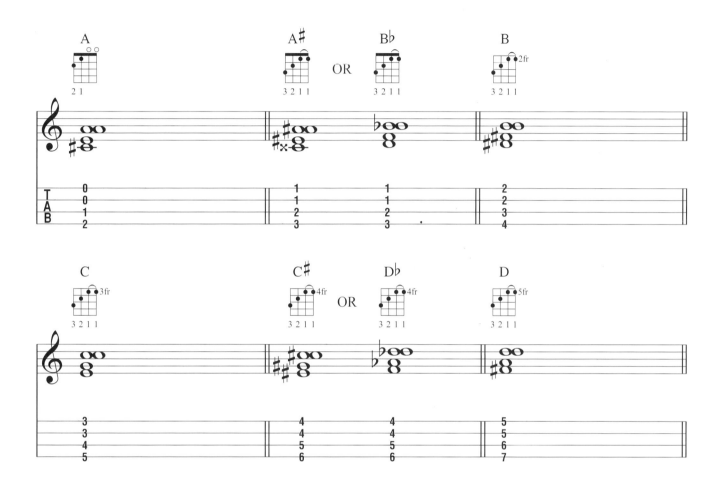

Vibrato

Vibrato will bring some life into your notes. Essentially, there are four different types of vibrato: fast, slow, small, and big. The technique of vibrato involves "shaking" a fretted note up and down off of its horizontal plane, creating a fluctuating, vocal-like effect. You can achieve this with any finger, but start with your 3rd finger on the 1st or 2nd strings. When using your 3rd finger, position your 2nd and 1st fingers behind your 3rd finger on the same string to provide strength and support. Blues guitar greats such as B.B. King, Stevie Ray Vaughan, and Albert King are some good players to listen to for vibrato ideas.

Be sure to check out the accompanying video tutorial and notation below for help with developing your vibrato.

Vibrato with 1st Finger

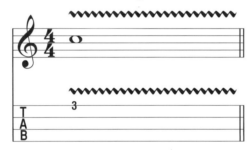

Vibrato with 3rd Finger

Bends ▶

The bending technique will add some energy and life to your notes, especially if you're into blues and rock. A *bend* is when you take a fretted note and "stretch" the string up to a higher note. Check out the video tutorial and notation examples.

There are three main bends for the ukulele: the quarter-step bend (1/4), half-step bend (1/2), and whole-step bend (1). Start with your 3rd finger on the 1st string, 5th fret; keep your 2nd and 1st fingers also down on the fretboard behind the 3rd finger for support.

A quarter-step bend is a subtle, slight string bend that doesn't quite reach the nearest pitch, but adds a nice, bluesy quality. It usually looks something like this in notation and tab:

Quarter-Step Bend

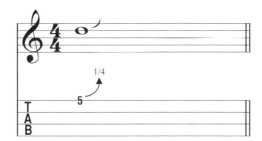

To create a half-step bend, for example, bend the note on the 1st string, 5th fret up so it sounds like the regular fretted note on the 6th fret. The note on the 6th fret is one fret, or one half step, up from the 5th-fret note. To play a half-step bend on the 5th-fret note, you'll want to aim for that target pitch on the 6th fret.

Half-Step Bend

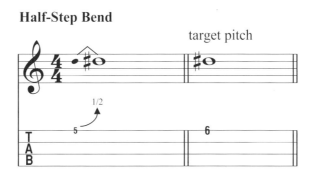

A whole-step (or "full") bend is when you bend a note the distance of two frets, or a whole step. For example, to play a whole-step bend on the 1st string, 5th fret, you would aim for the target pitch of the regular fretted note on the 7th fret.

Whole-Step Bend

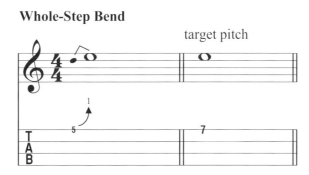

When practicing bends, play the fretted note you are trying to bend to first, so you have that pitch in your ear. You can also try adding vibrato to the top of your bends.

Whole-Step Bend with Vibrato

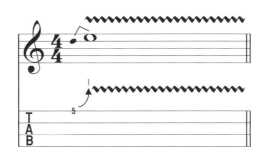

Congratulations! ▶

If you've made it through the course, congratulations! Come back to reference the book whenever you need to and keep enjoying your new ukulele skills!

Pro Tips & Info

Some ukulele greats to check out include:

- Israel Kamakawiwoʻole
- Jake Shimabukuro
- Roy Smeck
- George Formby
- Ukulele Orchestra of Great Britain

About the Author

Terry Carter is a San Diego–based ukulele player, surfer, songwriter, and creator of the #1 ukulele sites *ukelikethepros.com* and *store.ukelikethepros.com*.

With over 25 years as a professional musician, educator, and Los Angeles studio musician, Terry has worked with greats like Weezer, Josh Groban, Robby Krieger (The Doors), two-time Grammy-winning composer Christopher Tin (Calling All Dawns), Duff McKagan (Guns N' Roses), Grammy-winning producer Charles Goodan (Santana/Rolling Stones), and the Los Angeles Philharmonic.

Terry has written and produced tracks for commercials (Discount Tire and Puma) and TV shows, including *Scorpion* (CBS), *Pit Bulls & Parolees* (Animal Planet), *Trippin'*, *Wildboyz*, and *The Real World* (MTV). He has self-published over 10 books for Uke Like the Pros and Rock Like the Pros, filmed over 30 ukulele and guitar online courses, and has over 100,000 subscribers on his Uke Like the Pros YouTube channel.

Terry received a Master of Music in Studio/Jazz Guitar Performance from University of Southern California and a Bachelor of Music from San Diego State University, with an emphasis in Jazz Studies and Music Education. He has taught at the University of Southern California, San Diego State University, Santa Monica College, Miracosta College, and Los Angeles Trade Tech College.

Connect with Terry at *ukelikethepros.com*, *store.ukelikethepros.com*, and his social media channels including YouTube, Instagram, and Patreon.

Appendix A:
Notes on the Neck

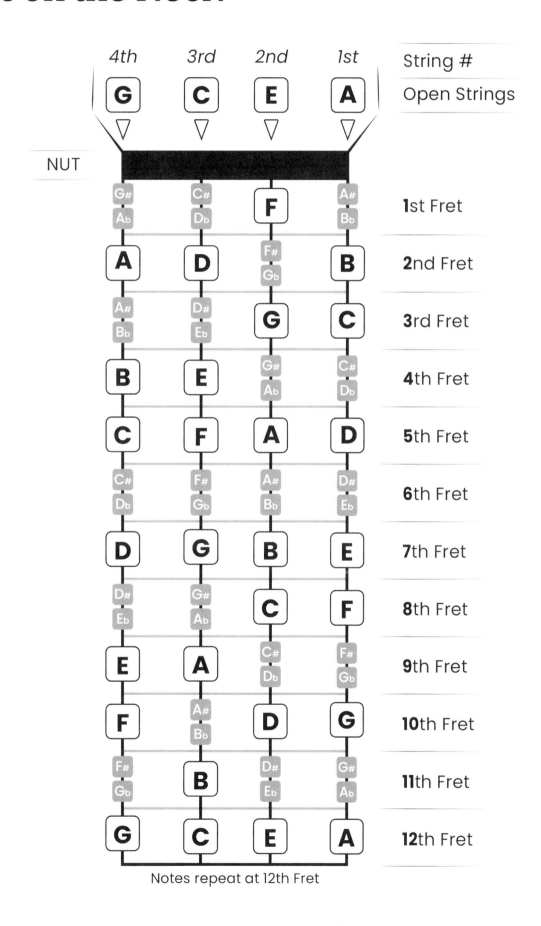

Notes repeat at 12th Fret

Appendix B:
Ukulele Chords

These are some of the most widely used ukulele chords in all of music. Although there are more chords than are shown here, these are the most common.

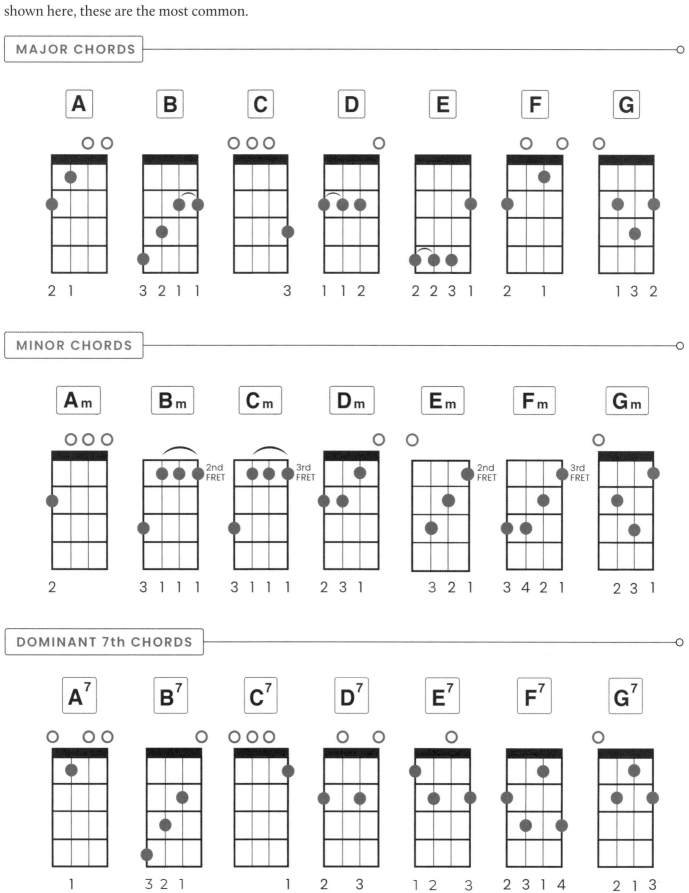

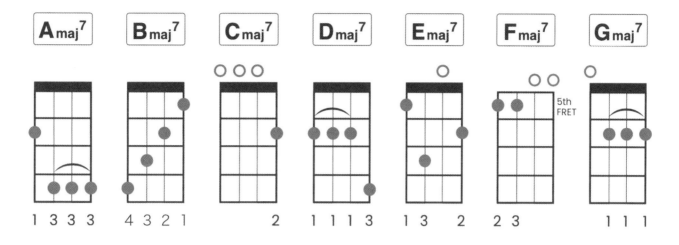

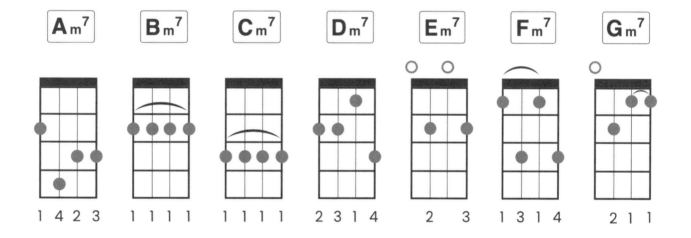

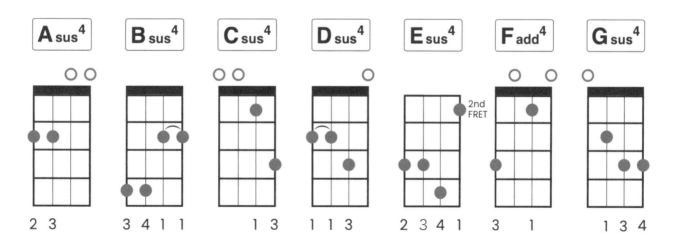

Appendix C:
Ukulele Notation Legend

THE MUSICAL STAFF shows pitches and rhythms and is divided by bar lines into measures. Pitches are named after the first seven letters of the alphabet.

TABLATURE graphically represents the ukulele fingerboard. Each horizontal line represents a a string, and each number represents a fret.

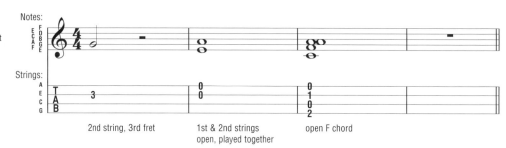

2nd string, 3rd fret

1st & 2nd strings open, played together

open F chord

HALF-STEP BEND: Strike the note and bend up 1/2 step.

WHOLE-STEP BEND: Strike the note and bend up one step.

GRACE NOTE BEND: Strike the note and immediately bend up as indicated.

SLIGHT (MICROTONE) BEND: Strike the note and bend up 1/4 step.

BEND AND RELEASE: Strike the note and bend up as indicated, then release back to the original note. Only the first note is struck.

PRE-BEND: Bend the note as indicated, then strike it.

VIBRATO: The string is vibrated by rapidly bending and releasing the note with the fretting hand.

HAMMER-ON: Strike the first (lower) note with one finger, then sound the higher note (on the same string) with another finger by fretting it without picking.

PULL-OFF: Place both fingers on the notes to be sounded. Strike the first note and without picking, pull the finger off to sound the second (lower) note.

LEGATO SLIDE: Strike the first note and then slide the same fret-hand finger up or down to the second note. The second note is not struck.

SHIFT SLIDE: Same as legato slide, except the second note is struck.

TRILL: Very rapidly alternate between the notes indicated by continuously hammering on and pulling off.

TREMOLO PICKING: The note is picked as rapidly and continuously as possible.

NOTE: Tablature numbers in parentheses mean:

1. The note is being sustained over a system (note in standard notation is tied), or

2. The note is sustained, but a new articulation (such as a hammer-on, pull-off, slide or vibrato) begins, or

3. The note is a barely audible "ghost" note (note in standard notation is also in parentheses).

Additional Musical Definitions

 (accent)

- Accentuate note (play it louder)

 (staccato)

- Play the note short

D.S. al Coda

- Go back to the sign (𝄋), then play until the measure marked "*To Coda*," then skip to the section labelled "**Coda**."

D.C. al Fine

- Go back to the beginning of the song and play until the measure marked "*Fine*" (end).

N.C.

- No chord.

- Repeat measures between signs.

- When a repeated section has different endings, play the first ending only the first time and the second ending only the second time.

UKULELE CHORD SONGBOOKS

This series features convenient 6" x 9" books with complete lyrics and chord symbols for dozens of great songs. Each song also includes chord grids at the top of every page and the first notes of the melody for easy reference.

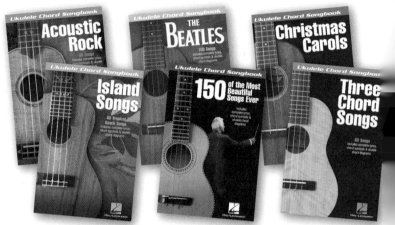

ACOUSTIC ROCK

60 tunes: American Pie • Band on the Run • Catch the Wind • Daydream • Every Rose Has Its Thorn • Hallelujah • Iris • More Than Words • Patience • The Sound of Silence • Space Oddity • Sweet Talkin' Woman • Wake up Little Susie • Who'll Stop the Rain • and more.
00702482 . . . . $15.99

THE BEATLES

100 favorites: Across the Universe • Carry That Weight • Dear Prudence • Good Day Sunshine • Here Comes the Sun • If I Fell • Love Me Do • Michelle • Ob-La-Di, Ob-La-Da • Revolution • Something • Ticket to Ride • We Can Work It Out • and many more.
00703065 . . . . $19.99

BEST SONGS EVER

70 songs: All I Ask of You • Bewitched • Edelweiss • Just the Way You Are • Let It Be • Memory • Moon River • Over the Rainbow • Someone to Watch over Me • Unchained Melody • You Are the Sunshine of My Life • You Raise Me Up • and more.
00117050 . . . . $16.99

CHILDREN'S SONGS

80 classics: Alphabet Song • "C" Is for Cookie • Do-Re-Mi • I'm Popeye the Sailor Man • Mickey Mouse March • Oh! Susanna • Polly Wolly Doodle • Puff the Magic Dragon • The Rainbow Connection • Sing • Three Little Fishies (Itty Bitty Poo) • and many more.
00702473 . . . . $17.99

CHRISTMAS CAROLS

75 favorites: Away in a Manger • Coventry Carol • The First Noel • Good King Wenceslas • Hark! the Herald Angels Sing • I Saw Three Ships • Joy to the World • O Little Town of Bethlehem • Still, Still, Still • Up on the Housetop • What Child Is This? • and more.
00702474 . . . . $14.99

CHRISTMAS SONGS

55 Christmas classics: Do They Know It's Christmas? • Frosty the Snow Man • Happy Xmas (War Is Over) • Jingle-Bell Rock • Little Saint Nick • The Most Wonderful Time of the Year • White Christmas • and more.
00101776 . . . . $14.99

ISLAND SONGS

60 beach party tunes: Blue Hawaii • Day-O (The Banana Boat Song) • Don't Worry, Be Happy • Island Girl • Kokomo • Lovely Hula Girl • Mele Kalikimaka • Red, Red Wine • Surfer Girl • Tiny Bubbles • Ukulele Lady • and many more.
00702471 . . . . $16.99

150 OF THE MOST BEAUTIFUL SONGS EVER

150 melodies: Always • Bewitched • Candle in the Wind • Endless Love • In the Still of the Night • Just the Way You Are • Memory • The Nearness of You • People • The Rainbow Connection • Smile • Unchained Melody • What a Wonderful World • Yesterday • and more.
00117051 . . . . $24.99

PETER, PAUL & MARY

Over 40 songs: And When I Die • Blowin' in the Wind • Goodnight, Irene • If I Had a Hammer (The Hammer Song) • Leaving on a Jet Plane • Puff the Magic Dragon • This Land Is Your Land • We Shall Overcome • Where Have All the Flowers Gone? • and more.
00121822 . . . . $14.99

THREE CHORD SONGS

60 songs: Bad Case of Loving You • Bang a Gong (Get It On) • Blue Suede Shoes • Cecilia • Get Back • Hound Dog • Kiss • Me and Bobby McGee • Not Fade Away • Rock This Town • Sweet Home Chicago • Twist and Shout • You Are My Sunshine • and more.
00702483 . . . . $15.99

TOP HITS

31 hits: The A Team • Born This Way • Forget You • Ho Hey • Jar of Hearts • Little Talks • Need You Now • Rolling in the Deep • Teenage Dream • Titanium • We Are Never Ever Getting Back Together • and more.
00115929 . . . . $14.99

Prices, contents, and availability subject to change without notice.

www.halleonard.com

Learn to play the Ukulele
with these great Hal Leonard books!

Hal Leonard Ukulele Method

Book 1
by Lil' Rev

The Hal Leonard Ukulele Method is designed for anyone just learning to play ukulele. This comprehensive and easy-to-use beginner's guide by acclaimed performer and uke master Lil' Rev includes many fun songs of different styles to learn and play. The accompanying audio contains 46 tracks of songs for demonstration and play along. Includes: types of ukuleles, tuning, music reading, melody playing, chords, strumming, scales, tremolo, music notation and tablature, a variety of music styles, ukulele history and much more.

00695847	Book Only	$8.99
00695832	Book/Online Audio	$12.99
00320534	DVD	$14.99

Book 2

00695948	Book Only	$7.99
00695949	Book/Online Audio	$11.99

Ukulele Chord Finder

00695803	9" x 12"	$8.99
00695902	6" x 9"	$7.99
00696472	Book 1 with Online Audio + Chord Finder	$16.99

Ukulele Scale Finder

00696378	9" x 12"	$8.99

Easy Songs for Ukulele

00695904	Book/Online Audio	$16.99
00695905	Book	$9.99

Ukulele for Kids

00696468	Book/Online Audio	$14.99
00244855	Method & Songbook	$22.99

Baritone Ukulele Method – Book 1

00696564	Book/Online Audio	$12.99

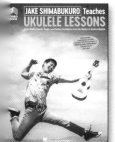

Jake Shimabukuro Teaches Ukulele Lessons

Learn notes, chords, songs, and playing techniques from the master of modern ukulele! In this unique book with online video, Jake Shimabukuro will get you started on playing the ukulele. The book includes full transcriptions of every example, the video features Jake teaching you everything you need to know plus video of Jake playing all the examples.

00320992 Book/Online Video $19.99

Ukulele Aerobics

For All Levels, from Beginner to Advanced
by Chad Johnson

This package provides practice material for every day of the week and includes an online audio access code for all the workouts in the book. Techniques covered include: strumming, fingerstyle, slides, bending, damping, vibrato, tremolo and more.

00102162 Book/Online Audio $19.99

Fretboard Roadmaps – Ukulele

The Essential Patterns That All the Pros Know and Use
by Fred Sokolow & Jim Beloff

Take your uke playing to the next level! Tunes and exercises in standard notation and tab illustrate each technique. Absolute beginners can follow the diagrams and instruction step-by-step, while intermediate and advanced players can use the chapters non-sequentially to increase their understanding of the ukulele. The audio includes 59 demo and play-along tracks.

00695901 Book/Online Audio $15.99

All About Ukulele

A Fun and Simple Guide to Playing Ukulele
by Chad Johnson

If you wish there was a fun and engaging way to motivate you in your uke playing quest, then this is it: All About Ukulele is for you. Whether it's learning to read music, playing in a band, finding the right instrument, or all of the above, this enjoyable guide will help you.

00233655 Book/Online Audio $19.99

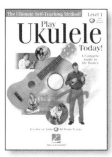

Play Ukulele Today!

A Complete Guide to the Basics
by Barrett Tagliarino

This is the ultimate self-teaching method for ukulele! Includes audio with full demo tracks and over 60 great songs. You'll learn: care for the instrument; how to produce sound; reading music notation and rhythms; and more.

00699638	Book/Online Audio	$12.99
00293927	Book 1 & 2/Online Media	$19.99

HAL•LEONARD®
www.halleonard.com

Learn to Play Today
with folk music instruction from Hal Leonard

Hal Leonard Bagpipe Method

The Hal Leonard Bagpipe Method is designed for anyone just learning to play the Great Highland bagpipes. This comprehensive and easy-to-use beginner's guide serves as an introduction to the bagpipe chanter. It includes access to online video lessons with demonstrations of all the examples in the book! Lessons include: the practice chanter, the Great Highland Bagpipe scale, bagpipe notation, proper technique, grace-noting, embellishments, playing and practice tips, traditional tunes, buying a bagpipe, and much more!
00102521 Book/Online Video $16.99

Hal Leonard Banjo Method – Second Edition

Authored by Mac Robertson, Robbie Clement & Will Schmid. This innovative method teaches 5-string, bluegrass style. The method consists of two instruction books and two cross-referenced supplement books that offer the beginner a carefully-paced and interest-keeping approach to the bluegrass style.
00699500 Book 1 Only...$9.99
00695101 Book 1 with Online Audio...............$17.99
00699502 Book 2 Only...$9.99
00696056 Book 2 with Online Audio...............$17.99

Hal Leonard Brazilian Guitar Method

by Carlos Arana

This book uses popular Brazilian songs to teach you the basics of the Brazilian guitar style and technique. Learn to play in the styles of Joao Gilberto, Luiz Bonfá, Baden Powell, Dino Sete Cordas, Joao Basco, and many others! Includes 33 demonstration tracks.
00697415 Book/Online Audio $17.99

Hal Leonard Chinese Pipa Method

by Gao Hong

This easy-to-use book serves as an introduction to the Chinese pipa and its techniques. Lessons include: tuning • Western & Chinese notation basics • left and right hand techniques • positions • tremolo • bending • vibrato and overtones • classical pipa repertoire • popular Chinese folk tunes • and more!
00121398 Book/Online Video $19.99

Hal Leonard Dulcimer Method – Second Edition

by Neal Hellman

A beginning method for the Appalachian dulcimer with a unique new approach to solo melody and chord playing. Includes tuning, modes and many beautiful folk songs all demonstrated on the audio accompaniment. Music and tablature.
00699289 Book..$12.99
00697230 Book/Online Audio...........................$19.99

Hal Leonard Flamenco Guitar Method

by Hugh Burns

Traditional Spanish flamenco song forms and classical pieces are used to teach you the basics of the style and technique in this book. Lessons cover: strumming, picking and percussive techniques • arpeggios • improvisation • fingernail tips • capos • and much more. Includes flamenco history and a glossary.
00697363 Book/Online Audio $17.99

Hal Leonard Irish Bouzouki Method

by Roger Landes

This comprehensive method focuses on teaching the basics of the instrument as well as accompaniment techniques for a variety of Irish song forms. It covers: playing position • tuning • picking & strumming patterns • learning the fretboard • accompaniment styles • double jigs, slip jigs & reels • drones • counterpoint • arpeggios • playing with a capo • traditional Irish songs • and more.
00696348 Book/Online Audio $12.99

Hal Leonard Mandolin Method – Second Edition

Noted mandolinist and teacher Rich Del Grosso has authored this excellent mandolin method that features great playable tunes in several styles (bluegrass, country, folk, blues) in standard music notation and tablature. The audio features play-along duets.
00699296 Book..$10.99
00695102 Book/Online Audio...........................$16.99

Hal Leonard Oud Method

by John Bilezikjian

This book teaches the fundamentals of standard Western music notation in the context of oud playing. It also covers: types of ouds, tuning the oud, playing position, how to string the oud, scales, chords, arpeggios, tremolo technique, studies and exercises, songs and rhythms from Armenia and the Middle East, and 25 audio tracks for demonstration and play along.
00695836 Book/Online Audio $14.99

Hal Leonard Sitar Method

by Josh Feinberg

This beginner's guide serves as an introduction to sitar and its technique, as well as the practice, theory, and history of raga music. Lessons include: tuning • postures • right- and left-hand technique • Indian notation • raga forms; melodic patterns • bending strings • hammer-ons, pull-offs, and slides • changing strings • and more!
00696613 Book/Online Audio $16.99
00198245 Book/Online Media $19.99

Hal Leonard Ukulele Method

by Lil' Rev

This comprehensive and easy-to-use beginner's guide by acclaimed performer and uke master Lil' Rev includes many fun songs of different styles to learn and play. Includes: types of ukuleles, tuning, music reading, melody playing, chords, strumming, scales, tremolo, music notation and tablature, a variety of music styles, ukulele history and much more.
00695847 Book 1 Only...$8.99
00695832 Book 1 with Online Audio...............$12.99
00695948 Book 2 Only...$7.99
00695949 Book 2 with Online Audio...............$11.99

HAL•LEONARD®

Visit Hal Leonard Online at
www.halleonard.com

Prices and availability subject to change without notice.